The Father Knows

Vernie McCoy

WESTBOW
PRESS®
A DIVISION OF THOMAS NELSON
& ZONDERVAN

Scripture taken from the King James Version of the Bible.

WestBow Press books may be ordered through booksellers or by contacting:

WestBow Press
A Division of Thomas Nelson & Zondervan
1663 Liberty Drive
Bloomington, IN 47403
www.westbowpress.com
1 (866) 928-1240

ISBN: 978-1-4908-8121-8 (sc)

Library of Congress Control Number: 2015907928

Print information available on the last page.

WestBow Press rev. date: 08/13/2015

Contents

Foreword

The 1500 questions that even Politicans, Scientists, Experts, and Judges, Teachers, Doctors and Lawyers can't answer. I challenge everyone of them to answer the questions about the "Thoughts of Truth" and practice what they preach.

Having knowledge is having the ability to do your work or job above the average person. However, an athletic person must be able to completely understand the game regulation and rules that he or she plays for the simple reason that is how a person advance to a higher position such as tennis, basketball, golf and football. We know that the ball must be in their court to have the advantage for a winning score.

These same people must be able to use their faith to soar high and produce some significant difference in the lives of individual they encounter everyday. The ruled must know about the Ruler in order to achieve success. These questions about the Ruler of the universe and accurate I must say at the least, please take the time to learn and share with others the information gained and know for certain it is the word of the Almighty God. Step out in faith. This is the Pentateuch, the first five books of the Old Testament. There are more than 1500 questions about these books. They have been researched to find the most interesting answers in the whole book.

The bible concerning some of the most topic people talk about every day. Please enjoy knowing that the things you say to people is the truth and can change individuals lives. Think about it that's what it is all about. Thank You! Enjoy talking with your friends about spiritual topics that are true and live today so they can have the advantage in life. Learning about Creation.

Knowing that God Almighty created the whole universe from the beginning.

This is the Pentateuch, the first five books of the Old Testament. There are more than 1500 questions about these books. They have been researched to find the most interesting answers in the whole book.

The bible concerning some of the most topic people talk about every day. Please enjoy knowing that the things you say to people is the truth and can change individuals lives. Think about it that's what it is all about. Thank You! Enjoy talking with your friends about spiritual topics that are true and live today so they can have the advantage in life. Learning abut Creation.

Knowing that God Almighty created the whole universe from the beginning.

Genesis chapters 1-50

Heaven and Earth

1. Who created heaven and earth? (GOD)
2. In the beginning, what was the condition of the earth? (The earth was without form and void, and darkness was upon the face of the deep.)
3. What moved upon the face of the waters? (The Spirit)
4. What did God say? ("Let there be light.")
5. Who saw the light? (GOD, and it was good.)
6. Who divided the light from the darkness? (GOD)
7. What did God call the light? (Day)
8. What did God call the darkness? (Night)
9. What was the first day? (The evening and the morning were the first day.)

10. What is the firmament? (Heaven)
11. What is the dry land? (Earth)
12. What were the waters called? (Sea)
13. Who made the grass? (GOD)
14. Who made every fruit tree and all other trees? (GOD)
15. What was made on the second day? (Heaven)
16. What was made on the third? (Grass and Trees)
17. Who made the seasons? (GOD)
18. God made two great lights? (Sun and Moon)
19. Who made the stars? (GOD)
20. What was made on the fourth day? (Sun, moon, and stars)
21. Who made water moving creatures and flying creatures? (GOD)
22. What day was it? (Fifth day)
23. Who made the living creatures and beasts of the earth? (GOD)
24. What great water living creature did God create? (Great whales)

Adam

25. Who made man in the image and likeness of God, having dominion over the fish of the sea, and over the fowl of the air, over the cattle and over all the earth, over every creeping thing that creepeth upon the earth? (GOD)
26. Who created male and female? (GOD created man in His own image, in the image of GOD created He him; male and female created He them.)
27. How did GOD bless them? (GOD said unto them be fruitful and multiply, and replenish the earth, and subdue it: and have dominion over the fish of the sea, and the fowl of the air, and over every living thing that moves upon the earth.)
28. What has been given us for food? (Herb bearing seed, which is upon the face of all the earth, and every tree, in which is the fruit of a tree yielding seed, to you it shall be for meat.)

29. What day was man created? (GOD saw everything that He had made, behold, it was very good. And the evening and the morning were the sixth day.)

30. What happen on the seventh day? (The heavens and the earth were finished, and all the host of them. On the seventh day GOD ended His work which He had made; and He rested on the seventh day from all His work which He had made.)

31. What do sanctified mean? (Set apart)

32. Why did GOD sanctified the seventh day? (He rested from all His work.)

33. Why was there no rain upon the earth? (There was no man to till the ground.)

34. Who was formed out of the dust of the ground? (Man)

35. What happened that man became a living soul? (GOD breathe into his nostrils the breath of life.)

36. Who planted a garden eastward in Eden? (The LORD GOD)

37. Who did the LORD GOD put in the garden? (The man, Whom He formed out of the dust.)

38. When the LORD GOD made the trees to grow. What trees were there in the garden? (Every tree that was pleasant to the sight and good for food.)

39. What other two trees was also in the garden? (In the midst of the garden were the tree of life and the tree of knowledge of good and evil.)

40. What was the name of four rivers in the garden? (Pison, Gihon, Hiddekel and Euphrates.)

41. What is in the land Havilah? (Gold)

42. What land did this river surround? (Ethiopia)

43. What river went toward east of Assyria? (Hiddekel)

44. Why was man put in the Garden of Eden? (Dress, and keep the garden.)

45. What tree did the Lord God command them not to eat freely thereof? (Tree of the knowledge of good and evil.)

46. Who named every living creature? (Adam)

47. Why did the Lord God caused a deep sleep to fall upon Adam? (He took one of his ribs, and closed up the flesh instead thereof.)

48. What was the rib used for? (He made a woman.)
49. What did Adam say about the woman that the Lord God had made? (She is bone of my bones, and flesh of my flesh: She shall be called Woman, because she was taken out of Man.)
50. Who shall leave father and mother and cleave to his wife? (Man)
51. Who were naked and not ashamed? (The man and his wife.)
52. How was the serpent different from other beast of the field? (The serpent was more subtle.)
53. Who was talking to the woman beside Adam and LORD God? (The serpent)
54. What did he say? Yea hath God said, ye shall not eat of every tree of the garden?
55. What did the woman know about eating out of the midst of the garden? (Ye shall not ear of it, neither shall ye touch it, lest ye die.)
56. What was the serpent reply? (Ye shall not surely die.)
57. What did the serpent know about God? (That His eyes were open and that He knew good and evil. That what made Him God.)
58. What can we learn from the woman about the tree? (The woman saw that the tree was good for food, and that it was pleasant to the eyes, and a tree to make one wise, she took of the fruit thereof, and did eat, and gave her husband with her; and he did eat.)
59. What happen? (The eyes of them both were opened, and they knew that they were naked; and sewed fig leaves together, and made aprons.)
60. What happen next? (They heard the voice of the LORD God walking in the garden in the cool of the day: And hid themselves from the presence of the LORD God amongst the trees of the garden.)
61. What did the LORD God call to Adam? (Where art thou?)
62. What did the man say to LORD God? (I heard thy voice in the garden, and I was afraid, because I was naked; and I hid myself.)
63. What was the LORD God answer to the Adam? (Who told you that thou were naked? Hast thou eaten of the tree, whereof I commanded thee that thou shouldest not eat?

64. Who did Adam say gave him of the fruit of the tree? (The woman that Thou gavest me, she gave me of the tree, and I did eat.)

65. What did the woman have to say? (The serpent beguiled me, and I did eat.)

66. The first punishment went to the very cause of the epic, the serpent. What was his punishment? (Thou are cursed above all cattle, and above every beast of the field: upon thy belly shall thou go, and dust shall thou eat all the days of thy life.)

67. What shall the LORD God put between the serpent's seed and the woman's seed? (Enmity)

68. What is enmity? (Hostility)

69. Who shall bruise the head? (The Woman shall bruise the head of the serpent.)

70. Who shall bruise the heel? (The serpent shall bruise the heel of the woman>)

71. What was judgment for the woman? (Greatly multiplied sorrow and conception; in sorrow bring forth children; and thy desire shall be to thy husband, and he shall rule over thee.)

72. What was Adam judgment? (You obeyed the voice of your wife, hast eaten of the tree, of which I commanded thee, saying, Thou shalt not eat of it: cursed is the ground for thy sake; in sorrow shalt thou eat of it all the days of thy life.

73. What shall the ground grow for man? (Thorns and thistles shall it bring forth to thee; and thou shalt ear the herb of the field.)

74. How shall man eat? (By the sweat of thy brow shall thou eat bread?)

75. What is man? (Dust)

76. What did Adam call his wife? (Eve)

77. What does Eve mean? (She was the mother of all living.)

78. Who made the first clothes? (LORD God)

79. What were the clothes made of? (Coats of skins)

80. What did the LORD God say man has become? (One of us, to know good and evil.)

81. What tree were they concerned about? (Tree of life)

82. What would happen if man eats of this tree? (Man would live forever.)

83. What did the LORD God do to man? (They drove man out of the Garden of Eden.)
84. What did the LORD God place at the east of the Garden of Eden? (Cherubim's and a flaming sword which turned every way.)
85. What was the purpose of the Cherubim's, and the flaming sword? (Keep the way of the tree of life.)
86. How did Adam and Eve become parents? (Adam knew Eve and she conceived.)
87. What was the first son name? (Cain)
88. What was the second son name? Abel)
89. What did Eve say about the first son? (I have gotten a man from the LORD.)
90. What was Abel job? (A keeper of the sheep)
91. What was Cain job? (A tiller of the ground.)
92. What would we call the men today? (Abel would be called a shepherd. Cain would be called a farmer.)
93. When it came offering time what did each man brings? (Cain brought of the fruit of the ground, and Abel brought the firstlings of his flock and of the fat thereof.)
94. Whose offering did the LORD have respect unto? (Abel)
95. Whose offering did He not have respect for? (Cain)
96. What is respect? (Paid attention)
97. Why was Cain wroth? (The LORD had not respect for his offering.)
98. Is Cain accepted? (NO)
99. What lied at the door? (Sin)
100. What did Cain do to Abel? (Slew him)
101. What did the LORD say about Abel's blood? (The voice of thy brother's blood cries unto me from the ground.)
102. What did the LORD set upon Cain? (A mark)
103. Where did Cain dwell? (The land of Nod, on the east of Eden.)
104. What was the name of Cain's first son? (Enoch)
105. Who was the father of the tent? (Jabal)
106. Who was the father of the harp and organ? (Jubal)

107. Who was the instructor of every artificer in brass and iron? (Tubalcain)
108. What other son did Adam and Eve have? (Seth)
109. What did Eve think about Seth? (God has appointed me another seed instead of Abel.)
110. When Seth had a son what did men began to do? (They began to call on the name of the LORD.)
111. How many years did Adam live? (One hundred and thirty years)
112. How old was Seth when he died? (Nine hundred and twelve)
113. Who was Enoch father? (Jared)
114. What was recorded about Enoch? (He walked with God: and was not; for God took him.)
115. Who was a Methuselah father? (Enoch)
116. How long did Methuselah live? (Nine hundred and sixty years)
117. Who was the father of Noah? (Lamech)
118. What did Lamech say about Noah? (This same shall comfort us concerning our work and toil of our hands, because of the ground which the LORD hath cursed.)
119. What does Noah mean? (Rest)
120. How old was Noah when he has his sons? (Five hundred years old)

The Sons of Noah

121. What were the names of Noah's sons? (Shem, Ham and Japheth)
122. What happen when men begin to multiply on the face of the earth? (The sons of God took them wives.)
123. Who are the sons of God? (Fallen spiritual being who corrupted the pre-Noah human race.)
124. What did the LORD say about man? (My Spirit shall not always strive with man, who is flesh, yet his days shall be a hundred and twenty years.)

125. What was in the land in those days? (Giants)
126. What did God note about man? (Every imagination of his thoughts of his heart was only evil continually.)
127. How did the LORD feel in His heart about man? (The LORD repented that He had made man on the earth, and it grieved Him at His heart.)
128. What did the LORD say about man? (I will destroy man from the face of the earth, both man, and beast, and creeping thing, and the fowl of the air.)

Noah

129. Who found grace in the sight of the LORD? (Noah)
130. What does the bible say about Noah? (He was a just man and perfect in his generations, and he walked with God.)
131. How were things on the earth in Noah days? (The earth was corrupt and filled with violence.)
132. What did God speak to Noah about? (Destroying all the flesh upon the earth.)
133. What was Noah instruction from God? (Make thee an ark of gopher wood. Rooms shall be in the ark and pitch it within and without pitch.)
134. What fashion did God tell Noah to make the ark? (The length of the ark shall be three hundred cubits, the breadth of it fifty cubits, and the height of it thirty cubits.)
135. What did he make in the ark that is what we still use today? (Window and door)
136. How many stories were there? (A lower, second, and third stories shall thou make it.)
137. How was God going to destroy the earth? (Flood)
138. What did God say He would make between Himself and Noah? (A Covenant)
139. Who would be in the ark? (Thou and thy wife and sons, and thy son's wives with thee.)

140. Who shall Noah bring into the ark with him besides his family? (Of every living thing of all flesh, two of every sort to keep them alive with thee, male and female.)

141. What did Noah need to take for his family and the beasts? (Food)

142. Did Noah obey God according to all he commanded? (Yes)

143. Why do you think that Noah was chosen by God? (Come into the ark, for thee have I seen righteous before me in this generation.)

144. How many shall Noah take of every clean beast? (Seven, male and female.)

145. How many shall Noah take of every unclean beast? (Two, male and female.)

146. How about the fowls of the air? (Seven, male and female.)

147. What did God speak to Noah seven days before the flood? (He would cause rain to fall upon the earth.)

148. How long would it be raining? (Forty days and forty nights.)

149. What was God destroying? (All living substance that He had made on the face of the earth.)

150. How old was Noah? (Six hundred years old.)

151. What month and day and year did the flood come? (In the sixth hundredth year, the second month, the seventeenth day of the month.)

152. What was happening? (The great deep broken up and the windows of heaven were opened.)

153. How high did the water increase? (The waters covered the hills and mountains.)

154. What dies at the flood? (All in whose nostrils was the breathe of life, died.)

155. How long were the waters upon the earth? (An hundred and fifty days.)

156. How did the flood stop? (God caused a wind to pass over the earth, and the waters subsided.)

157. What mountain did the ark rest on? (Ararat)

158. What bird did Noah sent to see if the waters was from the land? (Raven)

159. What was the second bird? (Dove)

160. Did she return? (Yes)

161. Why did the dove return? (She found no rest for the sole of her foot.)

162. How long before he sent her again? (Seven other days)

163. What did the dove have in her mouth? (An olive leaf.)

164. Did Noah get off the ark right then? (No he waited seven days more.)

165. When he sent the dove out again, did she return? (No)

166. What year and month did Noah return? (Six hundredth and first year, and the first month and the first day were the waters dried up from off the earth.

167. What was the month the earth dried? (The second month, on the seven and twentieth day of the month, was the earth dried.)

168. How did the LORD bless every living thing on the earth? (They may breed abundantly in the earth, and be fruitful, and multiply upon the earth.)

169. What did Noah build? (An altar)

170. What did Noah offering unto the LORD? (Noah took of every clean beast and every clean fowl, and offered burnt offerings on the altar.)

171. What did the LORD smell? (A sweet savor)

172. What did the LORD say in His heart? (I will not curse the ground anymore for man's sake.)

173. How is man's heart? (Evil from his youth)

174. What did He say about the earth? (While the earth remained, seedtime and harvest, and cold and heat, and summer and winter, and day and night shall not cease.)

175. What did God say to Noah and his sons? (Be fruitful and multiply, and replenish the earth.)

176. What did God tell Noah about the living creatures? (They shall fear and dread you.)

177. Was all that moveth upon the earth delivered into the hand of Noah? (Yes)

178. What is the meat for us? (Every moving thing that liveth and green herb.)

179. What kind of flesh shall we not eat? (Don't eat flesh with the blood in it.)

180. Why are we not to shed man's blood? (Man is made in the image of God.)

181. What is the token between God and every living creature upon the face of the earth? (A rainbow)

182. What does the rainbow reminds God of? (An everlasting covenant)

183. Where will the rainbow be? (In the cloud)

184. When God sees the rainbow, what will He remember? (The covenant)

185. What did Noah plant? (Vineyard)

186. What did he drink? (Wine)

187. Who covered their father? (Shem and Japheth)

188. Who didn't cover their father naked body? (Ham)

189. Did Noah curse Ham? (No)

190. Who was Ham father of? (Canaan,the generation that Noah cursed.)

191. Was Ham the oldest or the youngest? (Youngest)

192. What did Noah say about Ham? (A servant of servants shall he be unto his brethren.)

193. How did Noah bless Shem and Japheth? (God shall enlarge Japheth, and he shall dwell in the tents of Shem; and Canaan shall be his servant.)

194. How long did Noah live after the flood? (Three hundred and fifty years)

195. Who had a mighty hunter in the land? (Ham/Cush)

196. Did Nimrod have a kingdom? (Yes)

197. What is name of the great city? (Nineveh)

198. What cities were under Canaan? (Sodom and Gomorrah)

199. Who was thee eldest son? (Japheth)

200. Who built Nineveh? (Asshur)

201. Who was called a mighty hunter before the LORD? (Nimrod)

202. Who had the first kingdom? (Nimrod)

203. Who was Nimrod's father? (Cush)

204. Who was Cush's father? (Ham)

205. What did Noah say about Canaan? (Cursed be Canaan)

206. What else did Noah say about Ham generations? (A servant of servants shall he be unto his brethren.)

207. Who did Canaan begat at the first? (Sidon his first born and Heth)

208. What were families of the Canaanites? (Jebusite, and the Amorite, and the Girgasite, Hivite, Arkite, Sinite, and the Arvadite, and the Zemarite, Hamathite.)
209. What happen in the days of Peleg? (The earth was divided.)

Descendants of Shem

210. Who was Peleg's father? (Eber, Shem)
211. How was the whole earth? (The earth had one language and one speech.)
212. What did the people make that we still us today? (Brick and mortar)
213. What did the people decide to do? (To build a city, and tower.)
214. How far did they want the tower to reach? (Up to heaven)
215. What did they want to make for themselves? (A name)
216. What did they fear? (Being scattered aboard upon the face of the whole earth.)
217. Who came down to see the city and tower that man built? (The LORD)
218. What did the LORD say about the people? (The people are one, and one language, there is nothing restrained from them and what they imagine to do.)
219. What had to done to the people? (Let Us go down and confound their language, that they may not understand one another's speech.)
220. What happen afterwards? (They got scattered aboard upon the face of all the earth and they left off to build the city.)
221. What is the name of the city? (Babel)
222. What does the name Babel mean? (Confusion)
223. Who was Abram's father? (Terah)
224. Who was Terah's father? (Nahor)
225. Who were Abram's brothers? (Nahor, Haran)
226. Which one of Abram's brother was Lot father? (Haran)
227. What happen to Haran? (He died before his father in the land of his nativity.)
228. Who were their peoples? (Ur of the Chaldees)

229. What did Abram and Nahor do? (Took wives, Abram took Sarai and Nahor took Micah.)

230. What does the word say about Sarai? (She was barren.)

231. What is barren? (You have no child.)

232. Where did Terah die? (Haran)

233. How old was Terah? (Two hundred and five)

234. After Terah death, where did Abram dwell? (Canaan)

235. What did the LORD say to Abram? (Get away from thy father's house, I will make of thee a great nation and bless thee and make thy name great and thou shalt be a blessing.

236. What will happen to people that try to curse Abram? (I will bless them that bless thee, curse them that curse thee; in thee shall all the families be blessed.)

237. What land did Abram pass thru? (Si`chem., unto the plain of Moreh)

238. Who was in the land? (Canaanites)

239. Where did the LORD first appear to Abram? (Haran)

240. Where is the first place Abram built an altar? (The plain of Moreh)

241. Where is the first place Abram called on the name of the LORD? (Bethel of the west, and Haion on the east, there he built an altar.)

242. What does it mean to call on the name of the LORD? (To pray)

243. Who did start to call on the name of the LORD first? (Seth)

244. Which one of Noah's son was Abram father? (Shem)

245. Where did Abram go to after leaving Egypt? (He went to Bethel and Haion, the place where he has first made the altar and called on the name of the LORD.)

246. What was about the men of Sodom? (They were exceedingly wicked and sinners before the LORD, These people were the homosexuals in days gone by. See Roman chapt. 1:1-35)

247. Where did Abram move to after Lot went his separate ways? (He dwelt in the plain of Mamre.)

248. What is the value of Siddim? (Salt sea)

249. What is a vale? (Valley)

250. There was a war and it had slimepits. What is slimepits? (Tar pits)
251. What is the name of the first five books of the bible? (Genesis, Exodus, Leviticus, Numbers, Deuteronomy.)

Abraham

252. Who is the father of our faith? (Abraham)
253. What is the name of the promised son? (Isaac)
254. What is Abraham's wife name? (Sarah)
255. What is the name of Abraham's nephew? (Lot).
256. How old was Abraham and Sarah when Isaac was born? (Abraham was hundred years old and Sarah was ninety years old.)
257. How many years after Abraham left his father's house was Isaac born? (Twenty-five years later.)
258. What was Abraham's brother and his wife named? (Nahor and Milcah)
259. What was Abraham's father named? (Terah)
260. What was the land Abraham departed to? (Canaan)
261. What did the LORD appear to Abraham and say? ("Unto thy seed will I give this land.")
262. Whose house was Sarah taken into? (Pharaoh's house)
263. Why did they leave the place they were at? (Because of the famine)
264. Why did Abraham fear for his life on the way to Egypt? (Sarah was a fair woman, and he thought they would kill him for her.)
265. What did the LORD do to Pharaoh' house? (Plagued it).
266. In chapter 13 it tells us that Abraham was rich. What were his riches? (Silver
267. Why was the land not able to bear Abraham and Lot? (Their substance was great).
268. Which way did Lot go? (The plains of Jordon)

269. What was the name of the kings that made war in those days? (Amraphel, Arioch, Chedorlaomer, Tidal and Bera, Birsha, Shinab, Shemeber and Bela.)

270. Why did Abraham fight in the battle? (Because they had taken Lot and all his possession.)

271. How many trained servants did Abraham have? (Three hundred and eighteen)

272. Was Abraham successful in the war? (Yes)

273. Who was the king that went out to meet him. (King of Sodom)

274. What was the name of the king that brought forth bread and wine? (Melchizedek priest of the Most High God.)

275. What was Melchizedek reply to Abraham? (And he said Blessed be Abram of the Most High God, possessor of heaven and earth.)

276. What Abraham gives the king of Salem? (Tithes of all)

277. What did the king of Sodom ask for/? (Persons or people)

278. What was Abraham reply to the king of Sodom about the goods? (I will not take a thread or even a shoelatcket, or anything that is thine. You will not say you have made me rich.

279. Do you know what happen after these things? (The word of the LORD came to Abraham.)

280. What did the LORD say to Abraham about an heir? (His heir would come out of his own bowels.)

281. What do you think righteousness mean? (To believe God the Father.)

282. When God the Father cut a covenant with Abraham what animals did He tell Abraham to get? (A heifer of three years old and a she goat of three years old and a ram of three years old and turtledove and a young pigeon.)

283. Who was the first Preacher? (God the Father)

284. Who did He preach to? (Abraham)

285. What was some of the preaching's? (Unto thy seed I have given the land.)

286. How many years were his descendants to serve another nation? (Four hundred years.)

287. What was Sarah handmaiden name? (Hagar)

288. Where was she from? (Egypt)
289. Who give Abraham permission to go into her maid to obtain children? (Sarah)

Ishmael

290. What was the child named? (Ishmael)
291. How old was Abraham when Ishmael was born? (Fourscore and six years old, eighty-six)
292. How old was Abraham when he heard from God the Father again? (Ninety and nine years old)
293. What did the LORD say to Abraham? (I am Almighty God walk before me and be thou perfect)
294. Why did God change his name from Abram to Abraham? (Abraham means a father of many nations.)
295. What did God the Father say to Abraham about every male child? (Be circumcised)
296. How many days should they wait to circumcise the man child? (Eight days old)
297. What was Sarah name before and what does her new name mean? (Sarai, mother of nations)
298. Which son did God the Father say He will establish His covenant with? (Isaac)
299. How old was Ishmael when Abraham circumcise all in his household? (Thirteen)
300. Who appeared before Abraham in the plain of Mam're? (The LORD)
301. What foods did Abraham set before them? (A calf and bread, butter and milk.)
302. What cities was the LORD going to destroy? 9Sodom and Gomorrah)
303. Why was the cities to be destroyed? (Their sin grieved God)
304. Did Abraham try to stop Him from destroying the cities? (Yes)
305. How many righteous people would the LORD keep the city for? (Ten)
306. How many angels came to Sodom at even? (Two)

307. Who sat at the gate when they arrived? (Lot)
308. Who did they tell to go to the other city for protection? (Lot his wife and daughters.)
309. What kind of punishment did the cities receive? (Fire and brimstone)
310. What happen to Lot wife? (She looked back and became a pillar of salt.)
311. What did Lot's daughters think after the escape took place? (There is no man on the earth left but their dad.)
312. What did they made their father drink to preserve their father seed? (Wine)
313. What was the name of the king that took Sarah when they went to the south country? (Abimelech)
314. Did God the Father come to Abimelech in a dream? (Yes)
315. What did God the Father say to the king? (Behold, thou art but a dead man, for she is a man's wife.)
316. Did God the Father call Abraham a prophet? (Yes)
317. Why did Abraham have to pray to God the Father for Abimelech? (They had to be healed in order to bare children.)

Isaac

318. When Isaac was born what did Sarah say God the Father had made her do? (laugh)
319. Who voice did God here in the wilderness Hagar or the lad? (The lad, Ishmael)
320. Who did Abraham make a covenant with? (Abimelech)
321. How many lambs did he give the king as a witness? (Seven)
322. What was the name of the mountain that Abraham offered Isaac on? (Moriah)
323. What day was it as he entered the mountain? (The third day)
324. Did Isaac ask Abraham where is the lamb for the burnt offering? (Yes)
325. Who was the lamb for the offering? (Isaac)
326. Who called to Abraham out of the heaven? (An angel)

327. What did Abraham call the name of that place? (Jehovah-jireh)
328. What does Jehovah-jireh mean? (In the mount of the LORD it shall be seen)
329. How old was Sarah when she died (an hundred and seven and twenty years olds)
330. Where was Sarah buried? (Cave of Machpelah)
331. Where did Isaac's wife come from? (Nahor)
332. What was her name? (Rebekah)
333. Did Rebekah comfort Isaac after he mother had died? (yes)
334. Abraham took another wife, what was her name? (Ketura
335. How old was Abraham when he died? (An hundred and seventy-five)
336. How old was Ishmael when he died? (One hundred and thirty –seven)
337. How old was Isaac when he married Rebekah? (Forty year old)

Esau

338. What was the name of Rebekah twins? (Esau and Jacob)
339. How many wells did Isaac dig before he could have room for his family? (Three)
340. How old was Esau when he was married? (Forty years old)

Jacob

341. Who got the blessing from Isaac first? (Jacob)
342. What did Jacob see in his dream? (A ladder that set up on earth and reached to heaven: and behold angels of God the Father ascending and descending)
343. What was the name of the place where Jacob made a vow? (Bethel)
344. What did Jacob say he would give God for taking care of him? (A tenth unto Thee.)

345. What was the names of Jacob wives? (Leah and Rachel)

346. Who was the father of the twelve tribes of Israel? (Jacob)

347. How old was Isaac when he died? (One hundred and eighty years old)

348. What son did Jacob love the most? (Joseph)

349. What special thing did his father make for him? (A coat of many colors)

350. How many brothers did Joseph have? (Eleven)

351. Did the brothers of Joseph sell him to the Ishmaelite's? (Yes)

352. Was it Potiphar, an officer of Pharaoh who brought Joseph from the hand of the Ishmaelite's? (Yes)

353. What was Joseph accused of by Potiphar's wife? (Sexual assault)

354. How long did he stayed in the prison? (Two years)

355. Why was Joseph taken from the prison? (To tell Pharaoh his dream)

356. Did he become second in command? (Yes)

357. What was Joseph wife named? (Asenath)

358. What were his sons named? (Manasseh, Ephraim)

359. How old was Joseph when he stood before Pharaoh? (Thirty years old)

360. What was the name of Joseph's brothers? (Reuben, Simeon. Levi, Judah, Issachar, Zebulun, Gad, and Asher, Benjamin, Dan, Naphtali.)

361. Why was Joseph promoted to second in command? (He told Pharaoh the meaning of his dreams.)

362. What did Pharaoh say to Joseph about his wisdom? (A man in whom the Spirit of God is.)

363. What did Joseph reveal to Pharaoh about the famine? (The famine was soon to come)

364. What was Joseph plans about the outcome of the famine? (Let Pharaoh do this, appoint officers over the land, and take up the fifth part of the land of Egypt in the seven plenteous years.)

365. Who came to Joseph to get corn during the famine? (His brothers)

366. Did his brothers recognize Joseph? (No)

367. Did Joseph recognize his brothers? (Yes)

368. What was Joseph final response to his brothers? (Tears of Joy)
369. What was his brothers' response to him? (They were afraid that he would kill them)
370. How did Joseph treat them? (He had a kind heart knowing that God had sent him ahead of them to save their lives.)
371. What was Joseph ultimate feeling about the situation? (You meant it for evil, but God meant for my good.)
372. Jacob spoke a prophesy over all the brothers, what was some his prophesy over Joseph? (Joseph is a fruitful bough, even a fruitful bough by the well; whose branches run over the wall; you can read further in Gen. 49:22-26)
373. How old was Jacob when he died? (One hundred forty and seven years old)
374. Joseph was how old when he died? (One hundred and ten years old)
375. Did Joseph forgive his brothers after his father died? (Yes)
376. Who did Joseph say would visit the children of Israel? (God)
377. Did Joseph take an oath of the children ? (Yes)
378. What were they to do to his bones? (Carry them thence)
379. What does the name Genesis mean? (Beginning)

Exodus chapters 1-27

Hardship to Egypt

380. What does the name Exodus mean? (Journey)
381. How many months did Moses' parents hide him? (Three)
382. What was the decree in the land? (Kill all the males of the children of Israel.)
383. Who saved Moses alive? (Daughter of Pharaoh)
384. Did the daughter of Pharaoh pay Moses's mother to nurse him? (Yes)
385. How old was Moses when he fled from Pharaoh? (Forty)
386. What was Moses's sister and brother names? (Marion and Aaron)

387. Did he lead the children of Israel out of bondage? (Yes)

388. Did Moses see a burning bush ? (Yes)

389. How old was Moses at the time of his leadership? (Eighty)

390. How many plaques did he announce to the Egyptians? (Ten)

391. What nationality was Moses's wife? (Ethiopia)

392. What was her name? (Zipporah)

393. What was his son's name? (Gershom)

394. What did God say His name was? (I am who I am)

395. Who spoke to Moses out of the burning bush? (An angel)

396. What did the angel say to Moses ? (Take off your shoes, you are on holy ground)

397. What else did the angel say? (I am the God of thy father, the God of Abraham, the God of Isaac, and the God of Jacob.)

Redemption of Egypt

398. What did God want Moses to do ? (Bring forth my people out of Egypt)

399. What was the favor that God gave the people in the sight of the Egyptians? (Borrow jewels of silver and gold and raiment.)

400. What two signs did God give Moses to show His strength? (Moses rod became a serpent and his hand became leprous as snow.)

401. What was Moses response to God about his speech? (Slow tongue)

402. What did Moses and Aaron say unto Pharaoh? (Thus says the LORD God of Israel, Let me people go, that they may hold a feast unto me in the wilderness.)

403. Pharaoh said, Who is the LORD that I should obey His voice to let Israel go? (I know not the LORD; neither will I let Israel go. The LORD is the Gods of gods.)

404. What land was the LORD giving to the people of Israel? (Canaan Land)

405. Did Moses and Aaron do as the LORD commanded them? (Yes)

406. Did the LORD hardened Pharaoh Heart? (Yes)
407. Who did Moses and Aaron gather together? (All the elders of the children of Israel.)
408. Did the taskmasters force hard labor upon the people? (Yes)
409. What were the people made to do regarding brick? (To make their own bricks.)
410. What did the LORD say that He made Moses to Pharaoh? (God)
411. What did He make Aaron to Moses? (Prophet)
412. How old were Moses and Aaron when they led the people out of Egypt? (Moses were eighty and Aaron were eighty-three.)
413. What was the first miracle they showed to Pharaoh? (Take thy rod, and it shall become a serpent.)
414. What did Aaron's rod do to their rods? (Aaron's rod swallowed up their rods.)
415. How many days did the rivers and other bodies of water be filled with blood? (seven)
416. What was the next plaque on the Egyptians? (Frogs)
417. What was the fourth plaque? (Lice)
418. What was the fifth plaque? (Swarms of flies)
419. What is a grievous murrain? (Severe pestilence)
420. What was the next plaque? (Hail and fire mingled
421. What are the last three plaques? (Locusts, darkness and death of the firstborn)
422. What is the LORD's Passover? (A lamb of one year old roasted and its blood marked above the door post.)
423. What was the token of the blood? (To Passover every house with the blood over the door post.)
424. This day is a memorial to the Christians What is it called? (The Passover)
425. What shall they not eat for seven days? (Leavened bread)
426. Is the Passover an ordinance to be observe forever? (Yes)
427. What time of the night did the LORD smote the Egyptians? (Midnight)
428. How long did the children of Israel journey into Egypt? (Four hundred and thirty years)

429. Why must we observe the night the LORD brought the children of Israel of the land of Egypt? (The LORD brought them out with a strong and mighty hand. Great signs and wonders.)

430. How did the Lord lead the children of Israel by day and night? (A pillar of cloud by day and a pillar fire by night.)

431. What was the last thing that the LORD did to Pharaoh and his army? (They drowned in the Red Sea)

432. What instrument did the LORD use to part the Red Sea? (Moses' rod)

433. Did the children of Israel walk on dry ground? (Yes)

434. Did the people sing a song unto the LORD for that great victory? (Yes)

435. Do you think that this was the first song celebrating a wonderful victory in the bible of this kind? (Yes)

436. Who sang the song to the LORD? (Moses and the children of Israel.)

437. What instrument did the women use to celebrate this great victory? (Timbrel)

438. What did the women do today that we do to celebrate? (Dance)

439. Who lead the women into song and dance? (Miriam,the prophetess.)

440. Why do you think they called the LORD their song? (He was responsible for the victory.)

441. What shall we drink ? (After three days the people found water, but it was bitter and a tree made it sweet.)

Education of the redeemed in the wilderness

442. What was the statue and an ordinance that Moses made for them? (If thou wilt diligently hearken to the voice of the LORD thy God, and wilt do that which is right in His sight, and will give ear to His commandment, and keep all His statutes, I will put none of these diseases on thee, which I have brought on the Egyptians: for I am the LORD that healed thee.)

443. Why were the congregation of children of Israel murmuring against Moses and Aaron? (They were hungry.)

444. What did the LORD say He would rain from heaven? (Bread)

445. How much shall the people gather every day? (Certain rate every day)

446. How much shall they prepare on the sixth day? (Twice as much)

447. Was the bread from heaven called the LORD glory? (Yes)

448. What kind of flesh did the LORD give the children of Israel? (Quail)

449. What did they call the bread from heaven? (Manna)

450. What happen when they left the manna till morning? (It bred worms and stank.)

451. What was some of the requirements on the holy Sabbath? (Do not gather manna on the Sabbath and don't go out of place.)

452. What did the people do on the Sabbath? (Rest)

453. Describe the manna? (It was white coriander seed and the taste of it was like wafers made with honey.)

454. How many years did the children of Israel eat manna? (Forty years)

455. How much manna did the LORD tell Moses to save for the Testimony of generations? (An omer full of manna)

456. What measure if an omer? (Tenth of an ephah)

457. Why did the children of Israel chide with Moses at Rephidim? (They wanted water to drink.)

458. How did they get water this time?)Water came out of the rock when Moses smite it with his rod.)

459. What did the elders call the name of that place (Massah and Meribah)

460. Who fought with Israel in Rephidim? (Amalek)

461. When Moses held up his hand, that Israel prevailed: When he let it down who prevailed? (Amale)

462. When Moses hands got heavy, who held them up? (Aaron and Hur)

463. How long did they hold Moses hand up? (Till the sun went down.)

464. What did the LORD say He would do to the Amalek? (Put out the rememberance of the Amalek from under heaven,)

465. What name did Moses call the that place? (Jehovah-nissi)

466. What does that mean? (The LORD is my banner.)

467. Who was Jethro the priest of Midian? (Moses's father in law.)

468. What was one of Moses's son named? (Eliezer)

469. What does his name mean? (The God of my father was my help and delivered me.)

470. What does Gershom mean? (An alien in a strange land.)

471. When Moses told Jethro all that the LORD had done unto Pharaoh and the Egyptians. He rejoiced and blessed the LORD. What was Jethro words of gold from his heart? (Now I know that the LORD is greater than all gods: for in the thing wherein they dealt proudly He was above them.)

472. Did you know that Moses was a judge? (He judged the people from morning unto the evening.)

473. What counsel did Jethro, Moses's father in law give Moses? (Thou shall teach them ordinances and laws, and shall show them the way wherein they must walk, and the work that they must do.)

474. What kind of men did Jethro say that Moses shalt provide? (Able men such as fear God, men of truth, hating covetousness : to be rulers of thousands, and rulers over hundreds, rulers of fifties, and rulers of tens.)

475. Who shall Moses judge? (great matters)

476. Who and when shall the able men judge? (Small matters and all seasons)

477. Did Moses listen to his father in law? (Moses hearken to the voice of his father in law.)

478. Afterward what did God the Father say to Moses to speak to the house of Jacob, and the children of Israel? (Obey my voice indeed, and keep MY covenant ye shall be a peculiar treasure unto me above all people: for all the earth is Mine: Ye shall be unto me a kingdom of priests and an holy nation.)

479. What was the people reply to Moses speech? (And all the people answered together and said,. All that the LORD hath spoken we will do.)

480. How did the LORD say He would come to Moses? (I will come to thee in a thick cloud that he people may hear when I speak with thee, and believe thee forever.)
481. When God told Moses to sanctify the people what was He meaning? (To wash their clothes.)

Consecration of the Redeemed at Mount Sinai

482. What mount did God tell Moses to be ready for His visit? (Mount Sinai)
483. What day was He to approach them after they had washed their clothes or consecrated themselves? (The third day>)
484. What bounds did He set for the people not to touch? (Take heed to yourselves, that ye go not up into the mount, or touch the border of it>)
485. What would happen to the people if they touched the mount? (Whosoever touched the mount shall be surely put to death.)
486. What did Moses tell the husband? (Come not at your wives.)
487. What was happening when the people woke up? (There was thunder and lightning, a thick cloud upon the mount and the voice of the trumpet exceeding loud, so that all the people in the camp trembled.
488. What was happening on the Mount Sinai? (The mount was smoking as a furnace and the whole mount quaked greatly.)
489. What did the LORD tell Moses to do for the people? (Charge them no to gaze, and many of them perish.)
490. Why did the LORD tell Moses to get down to the people? (Only Aaron could come up with him.)
491. What was the reasoning's for the LORD speaking to the people? (To give them the Ten Commandments.)
492. Do you know the Ten Commandments? (Yes or No, You can find them at Ex. 20.)

493. What was the people response to God speaking to them on the Mount Sinai? (Fearful, thinking they would die.)

494. What are the different between commandments and judgments? (There are only Ten Commandments that tell us how to love God first and others and ourselves too. Judgment are a hundred telling us rules and regulations.)

495. What was the people response to the judgments? (All the people answered with one voice, and said, All the words which the hath said will we do)

496. Who wrote all the words of LORD? (Moses)

497. Who did Moses take with him after they made a covenant? (Aaron, Nadab and Abihu, and seventy of the elders of Israel>)

498. What did the LORD give Moses as he come up higher to the mount? (He gave him a tables of stone, and a law, and commandments which I have written: that thou may teach them.)

499. Who was Moses' minister? (Joshua)

500. How many days was Moses in the mount? (Forty)

501. What kind of heart do the LORD want an offering from? (Willing heart)

502. What is some of the offering that Moses could take? (Gold and silver and brass.)

503. What was the purpose of the offering? (To make a sanctuary for the LORD to dwell among them.)

504. What was the name of the angels for the tabernacle mercy seat? (Cherubim)

505. What was some of the pattern of the tabernacle? (Two cherubim of each side of the mercy seat.)

506. What did the ark of the testimony? (Table of shittim wood, mercy seat, and beaten gold and an overlay on the things,)

507. Who was first in the priest's office? (Aaron)

508. What was Aaron to wear? (Holy garments, for glory and beauty.)

509. Who was Aaron to minister to? The LORD)

510. What shall be a signet of pure gold? (A plate that says, HOLINESS TO THE LORD.)

511. What happen when something touches the alter? (It shall be holy.)
512. What is holiness? (Doing things God's way.)
513. How many times a year shalt thou keep the feast unto God? (Three times)
514. What feast shall the people keep and none shall stand before God empty? (Feast of Tabernacle)
515. How many times a year shall the males appear before the LORD? (Three times)
516. What will God send before thee to keep the in the way and to bring thee into the place which I have prepared. (An angel)
517. Who did God fill with the Spirit of God, in wisdom, and in understanding and in knowledge, and in all manner of workmanship? (Bezaleel the son of Uri, the son of Hur, of the tribe of Judah.)
518. Why did the people make the golden calf? (They thought Moses was not coming back.)
519. What was the calf made of ? (Gold earring)
520. The LORD wanted to consume the Israelites for what reason? (When they made a molten calf.)
521. Who wrote the Ten Commandments? (The tables was the work of God.)
522. Why did Moses brake the Ten Commandments? (His anger waxed hot, cause of the calf and dancing.)
523. What did Moses do with the calf? (He burnt it with fire, and ground it to powder, and strewed it.)
524. Moses said, Who is on the LORD side? (All the son of Levi gather themselves unto him.)
525. How many people fell that day? (About three thousands men.)
526. Which book was Moses talking about take his name out of? (Lamb book of life.)
527. What did Moses call the tabernacle? (Tabernacle of the congregation.)
528. How did the LORD speak to Moses? (Face to face as a man would speak to his friend)

529. What did Moses ask The LORD to show him? (His way)

530. Show me your glory? Said Moses. (You shall see my back parts, but my face you shall not see.)

531. Did the LORD write another ten commandments? (Yes)

532. What did the LORD say when He proclaimed His name? (The LORD, the LORD God, merciful and gracious, longsuffering, and abundant in goodness and Further can be read in Ex. 34:7)

533. What did Moses ask the LORD to do for them ? (Take them for an inheritance.)

534. What was the terrible thing the LORD would do for the people? (Drive out the other nations before them. Amorite, and Canaanite, and d the Hittite, and the Perizzite, and the Hivite, and the Jebusite.)

535. What did the LORD tell the people to do to their alters and images? (Destroy them and cut down their groves.

536. How did the LORD describe Himself referring to worship? (The LORD. Whose name is jealous, is a jealous God.

537. Who that openth the matrix is the LORD? (Every firstling among thy cattle whether ox or sheep.)

538. How many days has the LORD command that we work? (Six days and rest on the seventh day)

539. How did Moses's face look when he would come from the presence of the LORD? (His face shone and they was afraid of him.)

540. What did Moses have to do for the people to not be afraid? (Put a veil on his face)

541. What was one of the things that you could not do on the Sabbath day? (Kindle a fire)

542. What kind of heart was an offering taken from? (Willing heart)

543. What was the offering for ? (Tabernacle and sanctuary),

544. What was cloth of blue, and purple and scarlet for? (Holy garments for priests)

545. What was the cloud a symbol for? (The glory of the LORD)

Leviticus chapters 1-27

The Way of Access to God: Redemption

This is the book of Leviticus God will speak from the tabernacle that they made in Exodus. It is the third book of the pentacle. Let's follow the ways of God directing man to become as He is.

546. What offering is accepted by the LORD? (Offering of cattle, even of the herd, and of the flock.)
547. What shall they offer for a burnt sacrifice? (Offer a male without blemish.)
548. How shall the offering be offered? (His own voluntary offer.)
549. Where shall he offer it? (The door of the congregation, before the LORD.)
550. What is the offering for? (To make atonement for him.)
551. Where must the blood be sprinkle for an offering before the LORD and priests? (The blood must be sprinkle around the altar?)
552. Who shall flay the burnt offering? (The person who offer it.)
553. Who shall cut the offering into pieces? (The person who offer it.)
554. What does flay mean? (To strip the skin from by whipping.)
555. Who shall put the fire upon the altar, and lay the wood in order upon the fire? (The sons of Aaron the priest.)
556. How shall the sons of Aaron lay the parts upon the wood? (The head, and the fat, in order upon the wood athat is on the fire.)
557. How the inwards and legs be prepared? (His inwards and legs shall be wash in water.)
558. What shall the priests do next? (He shall burn all on the altar, to be a burnt sacrifice, an offering made by fire, a sweet savor unto the LORD.)
559. What kind of offering does He accept from the flock? (Sheep or goatsfor a burnt sacrifice, a male without blesmish.)

560. What side of the altar shall they kill the sacrifice? (Kill it on the northward side of the altar before the LORD, and the priests, Aaron's sons shall sprinkle his blood upon the altar.)

561. Will the LORD accept fowls for a burnt offering? (Yes)

562. What fowls are acceptable? (Turtledoves,or a young pigeons.)

563. How shall the priest burn it on the altar? (The priest shall bring it to the altar, wring off his head, and burn it on the altar.)

564. Where shall they put the blood? (The b lood shall be wrung out at the side of the altar?)

565. How shall the fowl feather be plucked? (He shall pluck his feathers, and cast it beside the altar on the east part, by the place of ashes.)

566. Do they divide the fowls? (They cleave it with the wings, not divide it asunder. The priests shall burn it upon the altar, upon the wood that is upon fire, an offering made by fire, a sweet savor unto the LORD.)

567. Do you know that a meat offering has no meat? (It is fine flour with oil upon with frankincense thereon.)

568. Do you know which offereing is most holy to the LORD made by fire? (Meat offering)

569. What are two items that should not be offered, made by fire? (Leaven bread, honey.)

570. Wfhat oblation should not be burn on the altar for a sweet savour? (Firstfruit)

571. What shall the meat offering be seasoned with? (Salt)

572. Should all offering be offer with salt? (Yes)

573. What is an example of firstfruit meat offering? (Green ears of corn dried by fire, beaten out of full ear.)

574. What oblation is a sacrifice of peace offering? (The herd of a male or female, without blemish before the LORD.)

575. Who do all the fat from animals belong to ? (All the fat is the LORD.)

576. What is a perpetual statue for your generations throughout all your dwellings? (Eat neither fat or blood.)

577. What way does the LORD want an offering from his people? (A cattle of herd, and of the flock, of his own voluntary will.)
578. What is this king of offering for? (Atonement for sin)
579. What is a burnt offering? (A male of the herd, without blemish, at the door of the tabernacle)
580. What is a sin offering? (A young bullock without blemish unto the LORD.)
581. What is an atonement? (Reconciliation)
582. What does it mean to be anointed? (Rub oil on, carry in the temple of the LORD's His awesome power.
583. What does it mean to be forgiven? (Pardon)
584. What is a trespass offering? (Soul swear)
585. What is it to be unclean? (Touch a carcass of a unclean thing)
586. What is unleavened bread? (Bread without yeast)
587. What is an abomination? (Detestable)
588. What is an ephods (priestly robe)
589. What is a mitre? (Turban)
590. What is Urim and Thummim? (Light and Perfection)
591. What is a sweet savor? (Soothing aroma)
592. What are some unclean beast that we should not eat? (Camel, Coney, hare and swine is unclean to us.)
593. Of the waters, what shall we eat? (Whatsoever hath fins and scales)
594. God called some things in the rivers an abominations. Why? (No fins or scales is an abomination to us.)
595. Among the fowls. What is an abomination to us? (The eagle, and the ossifrage and the ospray, the vulture, kite, raven, owl, hawk, cuckow, cormorant, swan and the pelican,stork,the heron, lapwing and the bat. All fowls that creep going upon all four, shall be an abominate
596. What creeping thing may we eat? (Locust, bald locust, beetle and the grasshopper)
597. What are some of the unclean beast? (Weasel, mouse, and tortoise, ferret and the chameleon, lizard, and snail and the mole.)

598. Concerning the birth of a male child, what are we supposed to do to stay clean? (Be separated according to her period for seven days.

599. After birth of a man child the woman shall continue how many days in her purifying be fulfilled? (Three and thirty days)

600. How many weeks if she bear a maid child. (Two weeks as in her separation: and she shall continue in the blood of her purifying three-score and six days.)

601. When a man shall have in the skin his flesh a rising, and scab, or bright spot, and it be in the skin of his flesh, what is this called? (Leprosy)

602. What must he do? (Go show himself to the priest and offer an offering.)

603. What will the priest do to pronounce the man clean? (One of many things must be done to cleanse the person of leprosy. An offering, wash his clothes, and anoint with oil. Other things are mentioned at Lev. 13 & 14

604. When offering a burnt offering, what are they instructed not to do with the blood of the animals? (Don't eat any manner of blood.)

605. There are severals reason why a man will be cut off from among his people. Can I name one of them? (Yes, to kill an ox, or lamb, or goat, in the camp, or that killeth it out of the camp, and bringeth it not unto the door of the tabernacle of the congregation, to offer an offering unto the LORD before the tabernacle of the LORD; blood shall be imputed unto that man: he hath shed blood; and that man shall be cut off from anmong his people.)

The Way of Living for God: Holiness

606. What does the blood do for the soul? (The blood makes an atonement for the soul.)

607. What is in the blood? (The life is in the blood.)

608. What was expected of the people to understand about the blood? (No soul can eat blood.)

609. If any person catched an beast or fowl he must know to do this? (Pour out the blood and cover it with dust.)

610. Can a person eat an animal that die of itself? (Yes but it does make that person unclean even until the evening, he must wash his clothes and take a bathe.)

611. What happens when that person does not wash his clothes or take a bathe? (He will have to bear his iniquity or guilt.)

612. What has the LORD asked us to do, because He is the LORD our God? (Do my judgments, keep mine ordinances, to walk thereina; keep my statues and judgments. I am the LORD thy God.)

613. What is the first thing listed that a man should not do to any kin person? (None of you should approach to any that is near of kin to him to uncover their nakedness: I am the LORD.)

614. What does lie carnally mean? (To have intercourse

615. What does it means to uncover their nakedness? (To lie with any of the kin is an abomination with the LORD. He has drove out the people that did this same thing before that live in the land before the Israel came into that land.)

616. What is it called when one person lie carnally or uncover the nakedness of more than one member of his family, even in laws? (This is a sinful act called wickedness.)

617. If any person lie with a beast, it is an abomination and ? (It is confusion.)

618. What happens when the land is defiled? (The LORD says he visit the land and it vomited out the habitatants.)

619. What have we learned that man do to defile the land? (Abominations defile the land.)

620. How does the lands react to abominable things? (The land spew out the abominable things.)

621. What is spewing? (Vomiting)

622. What happen to the nations before Israel? (They got spewed out of the land.)

623. Have we seen spewing of the land? (Yes, earthquakes and tsunamis.)

624. Why is it an abomination for mankind to lie with mankind, as with a woman? (They cannot reproduce and there will be no generations coming forth to the earth, seedtine and harvest must be here on the earth while the earth remaineth.)

625. What does cut off from among the people mean? (To be destroyed.)

626. What have God called us to be ? (Holy)

627. How can we be holy? (Doing His commandments, statutes, ordinances, judgments and laws.)

628. What is one thing we must do for our mothers and fathers? (Fear every man his mother and father and keep the sabbaths.)

629. What should we not make before the living God? (Images of molten gods for worship.)

630. When will the LORD not accept a peace offering? (When the offering must be eaten on the first day. It is not acceptable to keep it till the third day.)

631. Who is Molech? (The god that they sacrifice children too)

632. Why should you not gleam all the harvest? (The corner must be left for the poor and stranger.)

633. Why was the people asked not to go after familiar spirits and wizards? (The LORD will set His face against the people and cut them off from among their people,)

634. Why was they asked not to curse their parents? (The other nations did it before them and it was wrong.)

635. Who is an adulterers and an adulteress? (A man or woman who lies with their neighbor's wife.)

636. What is the punishment for adultery? (To be put to death.)

637. Why should a man not lie with his daughter in law? (It is an abomination, and wrought confusion.)

638. What happen when a man takes his brother's wife? (They should be childless.)

639. Who shall a priest take to wife? (A virgin of his own people.)

640. Which priest should not offer bread to the LORD? (A man with a blemish.)

641. Can a priest, that is a leper eat the holy things ? (No)

642. Can a unclean priest touch the holy things of the LORD? (No)

643. When can the priest eat the food? (Take a bath and when the sun goes down he may eat.)

644. Name severals people who may not eat of the holy things? (Strangers and Sojourners or hired servants).

645. When can a priest's daughter not eat holy things? (If she marry a stranger.)

646. Name some circumstances when the priest daughter can eat? (She be a widow, or divorced and have no child, and returned unto the father's house in her youth, she may eat at her fathers house.)

647. Would you offer a blind, or broken, or mained, or having wen orf scurry, or scabbd, unto the LORD. (No, it is unacceptable.)

648. Do you offer a bullock or a sheep that has anything superfluous for a freewill offering? (Yes, but not for a vow.)

649. Do you offer that which is bruised or crushed, or broken or cut? (No, neither make any offering thereof in your land.)

650. Will a bullock, or sheep and goat be accepted? (Yes)

651. What is a dam? (It mean mother)

652. How old must the bullock, sheep or goat be? (Eight days old will be accepted.)

653. Can you kill the cow or ewe and her young all in one day? (NO)

654. How should you offer a thanksgiving sacrifice? (Your own freewill.)

655. When shall the offering be eaten> (The same day, none of it shall be left.)

656. Who shall the LORD be hallowed among? (The children of Israel.)

657. What does hallowed mean? (Sanctified)

658. What will happen if your son or daughter curse God? (They shall bear their iniquity.)

659. What will happen if you sow a field on the sixth year and on the seventh you do not sow? (It shall be a sabbath rest.)

660. Can you sow a field or prune a vineyard? (No)

661. What is the land called when you have forty and nine years? (Jubilee)

662. What year will the LORD command His blessing? (Sixth)

663. How many years will it bring forth fruit? (For three years)

664. When will the LORD have covenant with Jacob, Isaac, Abraham? (If they shall confess their iniquities and the iniquities of their fathers, with their trespasses which they trespassed against Me, and that also they have walked contrary unto Me, and that I also have walked contrary to them and have brought them

into the land of their enemies; if their uncircumcised heart be humbled and they accept the punishment of their iniquities.)

The Way of Living For God: Holiness

665. What is in the blood? (Life)

666. What was the purpose of the blood? (To make an atonement for the soul.)

667. What did the LORD say about not approaching near of kin? (Not to uncover their nakedness, or lie with a relative, incest forbidden)

668. What about same sex? (Thou shall not lie with mankind, as with womankind: it is abomination.)

669. What is not a surprise that man should not lie with? (Beast)

670. What is the LORD ordinances? (Laws)

671. What did the LORD say would happen to the soul that sinned? (They shall be cut off from among their people.)

672. Is anything too hard for the LORD? (No)

673. The LORD say be holy even as I am holy what does that mean? (Right standing with God.)

674. What does it mean to revered thy father and mother? (Fear them)

675. What did the LORD say to Moses about the congregation of the children of Israel? (Take you the sum of the children of Israel.)

Numbers chapters 1-36

676. What was the youngest person age? (Twenty years old and up.)

677. What must they be able to do? (Able to go forth to war.)

678. What else did He ask Moses to do? (A man from every tribe.)

679. Describe the name of the tribe and the men? (Tribe of Reuben; Elizur the son of Shedeur. Of Simeon; Shelumiel the son of Zurishaddai, Of Judah; Nahshon the son of Amminadab, Of Issachar; Nethaneel the son of Zuar, Of Zebulun; Eliab the son of Helon, Of the children of Joseph: of Ephrain; Elishama the son of Ammihud::: of Manasseh; Gamaliel the son of Pedahzur, Of Benjamin; Abidan the son of Gideoni, Of Dan; Ahiezer the son of Ammishaddai, Of Asher; Pagiel the son of Ocran, Of Gad; Eliasaph the son of Deuel, Of Naphtale: Ahira the son of Enan.)

Prepartion For Leaving Mount Sinai

680. Where did the numbering of the name take place? (Wilderness of Sinai)
681. What group of people did the LORD not name? (Levites)
682. How did the LORD tell Moses to number the children of the Levites? (A month old and upward, shall thou number them,)
683. What was the name of the families? (Gershonites)
684. Who was the chief of the house? (Eliasaph, the son of Lael.)
685. What was their charge? (The ark, and the table, and the candlestick, and the altars, and the vessels of the sanctuary, wherewith they minister, and the hanging, and all the service thereof.)
686. What did the LORD say about the Levites? They are mine, sayeth the LORD.)
687. What amount of money is the shekel? (A shekel is twenty gerahs.)
688. Who was to receive the money for the redeemed people? (Aaron and his sons.)
689. What age should Moses take the sum of for the work of the tabernacle? (From thirty years old to fifty years old.)
690. What did the LORD command Moses to tell the children of Israel? (To put out of the camp the lepers and them that had an issue, and defiled of the dead.)
691. What is a vow of a Nazarene? (To separate them self from wine and strong drink, no shave the head.)

692. What else would a Nazarene do? (Let their hair grow on the head.)

693. If he shall touched a dead body what should be done? (He shall shave his head.)

694. On what day shall he shave his head? (Seventh day)

695. On what day shall he bring two turtledoves and two young pigeons to the priest to the door of the of the tabernacle of the congregation? (Eighth day)

696. What are the two offering the priest shall offer? (Sin and burnt offering)

697. What will this do for him? (An atonement)

698. What shall the lamb of the offering be? (An lamb of the first year for a trespass offering.)

699. What happen if a man's wife commit a trespass against him? (He shall bring her to the priest and make an offering for her.)

700. What shall be the offering for the wife? (The tenth part of an ephah of barley meal.)

701. What is the offering called? (Jealousy offering)

702. What else is the offering called? (Bringing iniquity to remembrance.)

703. When the woman is found guilty, what do the priest tell the woman? (The LORD make thee a curse, and cause thy belly to swell and thy thigh to rot.)

704. What happens when the woman is clean? (Then she shall be free, and shall conceive seed)

705. What did each prince offer to the LORD on his day? (They each offered silver and gold, rams, goat and lambs, oxen and fine flour mingled with oil and incense.)

706. How many days did this offering take place? (Twelve days)

707. When the offering was completed Moses heard someone speaking to him from where? (Off the mercy seat upon the ark of the testimony, from between the two cherubim.)

708. Who do you suppose the voice were? (The LORD)

709. What is the age requirement of the Levites? (From twenty-five and upward they shall go in to wait upon the service of the tabernacle of the congregation.)

710. What is the age requirement of the Levites? (From fifty years they shall cease waiting, and serve no more.)

711. What did the Lord say about the Passover? (Keep it at its appointed season.)

712. What day was it appointed? (The fourteenth day of the first month)

713. What did the LORD say about unclean men who wanted to keep the Passover? (They could eat it with unleavened bread and bitter herbs, leave none of the food until the morning for break any bone of it.)

714. When the tabernacle was reared up the cloud covered the tabernacle what part namely was covered? (The tent of the testimony.)

715. What always covered the tent and tabernacle? (The cloud covered it by day, and the appearance of fire by night.)

716. When the cloud was taken up what happened? (They journeyed)

717. When the cloud tarried what happened? (The children of Israel abode.)

718. Did the children of Israel keep the commandment of the LORD? (They kept the charge of the LORD)

719. What did the LORD tell Moses to make two trumpets for? (For calling of the assembly, and for the journeying of the camps)

720. What did He say they should be made of ? (Silver)

721. When they blow one trumpet what shall happen? (The princes, which are the heads of the thousands of Israel shall gather themselves unto thee.)

722. Who was Raguel? (He was a Midianite)

723. What did Moses say to him? (I will give it to you.)

Wilderness wamderings

724. Why did Moses ask him to go with them? (He knew how to encamp in the wilderness.)

725. Did Raguel stay with them? (He said I will depart to mine own land.)

726. How many days journey did the go to find a resting place? (Three days journey)

727. What happen when the people complained? (The fire of the LORD burnt among them, and consumed them.)

728. What was some of the foods the Israelites eat in Egypt? (Fish, cucumbers and melons and the leeks and the onions and garlic.)

Wilderness Wonderings

729. What was manna? (Coriander seed)
730. When did manna fall? (When the dew fell upon the camp at night.)
731. How many men did Moses have to gather for the LORD ? (Seventy men
732. What did the LORD ask Moses "Is the LORD's hand waxed short? (Thou shall see if my words shall come to pass or not.)
733. Did the LORD words come to pass? (Yes)
734. What flesh did the Lord bring into the camp? (Quail)
735. What was the name of that place? (Kibrothhattaavah)
736. Why was it called Kibro that taavah? (They buried the people that lusted.)
737. Where did they journey to next? (Hazeroth)
738. Why did Miriam and Aaron speak against Moses? (His wife was Ethiopian.)
739. Who heard it and was worth? (The LORD)
740. How did the LORD come down? (In a pillar of a cloud.)
741. Who did the LORD say calls the prophets or makes them? (I the LORD will make me known unto them.)
742. How did the LORD say he speaks to the prophet? (In a vision and a dream.)
743. How did the LORD say that Moses was different? (He spoke to Moses face to face or mouth to mouth.)
744. What did Miriam become? (Leprous)
745. What did Aaron say unto Moses? (Lay not our sin upon us, wherein we have done foolishly and sinned.)
746. How many days did Miriam have to stay away from the camp? (Seven days)
747. What nationality was Moses' wife? (Ethiopian)
748. What happen to Aaron? (Nothing has happen yet.)

749. Why do you think nothing happen yet? (Aaron is a priest)

750. Who called out to the LORD to save Miriam? (Moses)

751. How did the bible describe Moses's behavior? (Now Moses was very meek above all the men of the face of the earth.)

752. What did the LORD say about her father? (If he had spit in her face, she would be ashamed seven days.)

753. What area was covered when the men spied the land? (The wilderness of Zin unto Rehob)

754. Why did they cut the grapes down? (Brook of Eschol)

755. What other kind of fruit did they find? (Pomegranates and figs.)

756. How many days did they search the land? (Forty days)

757. What did the men say that the land flowed with? (Milk and honey)

758. How did they describe the people of the land? (Strong)

759. How did they describe the cities? (The cities are walled and very great.)

760. Who dwelled where in the land? (The Am'a–lek-ites dwell in the south: Hittites, Jebusites, and the Amorites dwell in the mountains: Canaanites dwell by the sea, and by the Jordon.)

761. Who stilled the people before Moses? (Caleb)

762. What did he say? (Let us go up at once and possess it; for we are well able to overcome it.)

763. What did the other men say that went up with them? (We are not able to go up against them, for they are stronger than us.)

764. What kind of report did the men who spied out the land bring up? (An evil report)

765. Who disagreed with the report? (Caleb and Joshua)

766. What stature of men did the spy see? (Giants)

767. When the people heard the report what was their response? (The people wept that night.)

768. How did the people handle the situation? (They murmured against Moses and Aaron.)

769. How many people murmured? (The whole congregation complained.)
770. What did they decide to do? (They decided to return to Egypt.)
771. What did they suggest to do? (To make a captain)
772. What did Moses and Aaron do before all the assembly of the congregation? (They fell on their faces.)
773. What two men brought up a good report? (Joshua and Caleb)
774. Why did they rent their clothes? (The people was fearful and angry.)
775. Who was with the people ? (The LORD.)
776. Did the people have a reason to complain or murmur? (No)
777. Why would we not complain ? (We know that you must have faith in the heart.)
778. How would we get that faith? (Simply meditating on the word of God.)
779. What word did they have to meditate on ? (The ten plaques for starters.)
780. What did the people want to do to Moses and Aaron? (The wanted to stone them.)
781. What happen when this situation occurred? (The glory of the LORD appeared in the tabernacle.)
782. How did they anger the LORD? (They did not believe Him.)
783. What had the LORD determine to do to them? (The LORD said He would smite them with pestilence and disinherit them, and make a nation greater and mightier than them.)
784. What did Moses have to say about the LORD new plans for the people? (The Egyptians will hear and tell the other inhabitants that the LORD was not able to bring this people into the land which He swore unto them, therefore He hath slain them in the wilderness.)
785. Why was Moses so good at talking to the LORD about not slaying the people in the wilderness? (He spoke the LORD own words to Him and saved the people life.)
786. What did Moses say? (Pardon, I beseech Thee, the iniquity of this people according unto the greatness of Thy mercy, and as Thou hast forgiven this people, from Egypt even until now.)

787. Did the LORD of all creation listen to Moses? (Yes)

788. How did Moses accomplish such a great milestone? (Reminding the LORD of His own words)

789. What did the LORD of all creation say about the earth? (The earth shall be filled with His glory.)

790. What did the LORD say about the people that did not believe Him? (They would not see the Promised Land.)

791. What man did He say would be welcomed into the Promised Land? (Caleb)

792. Who would have to bear their iniquities? (Everyone from twenty and upward.)

793. What other man did the LORD make welcomed into the Promised Land? (Joshua)

794. Who did the LORD say would come in also? (The little ones)

795. How many years would they wonder in the wilderness? (Forty years)

796. How many days shall they bear the own iniquities? (A day for a year, even forty years.)

797. How did the men that brought up the evil report die? (Plaque)

798. When the people rose up early in the morning where did they go? (Into the mountain)

799. What did the people do when Moses told them what the LORD had said? (Mourn greatly)

800. When they decided to engage into battle despite what the LORD told them to do what happen? (Moses said the LORD is not with you, it shall not prosper.)

801. Did the people listen to Moses? (No)

802. What happen to them? (The Ark of the Covenant departed not out of the camp.)

803. Who battled against Israel? (The Amalekites and the Canaanites smote them even to Hormah.)

804. What are some the offerings that should be brought to the LORD? (Make an offering by fire unto the LORD)

805. When the people come to where the LORD tell them what offering is acceptable? (Heave offering)

806. What shall happen if you err in giving the LORD your offering? (Then all the congregation shall offer one young bullock for a burnt offering, for sweet savor unto the LORD with his meat offering and his drink offering, according to the manner, and one kid of the goats for a sin offering and the priest shall make an atonement for all the congregation of the children of Israel and it shall be forgiven them.)

807. What happened to the man that gathered sticks on the Sabbath day? (He was stoned.)

808. What do they have to make on the borders of their garments? (Fringes)

809. What is the purpose of the fringes? (To look upon and remember all the commandments of the LORD and do them.)

810. What does doing the commandments make a person? (Holy)

811. What were the names of the men that gather against Moses? (Korah, Dathan, and Abiram)

812. What did he accuse Moses of doing? (Lifting himself up against the congregation.)

813. How many men came together against Moses and Aaron? (Two hundred and fifty princes.)

814. What happen to these men? (The earth swallow them and their houses and all the men that appertained unto Korah.)

815. Where did they go ? (In the pit.)

816. Why did Israel fled round about them? (They thought the earth would swallow them up too.)

817. Who took up the censers? (Eleazar, son of Aaron)

818. How many rods were they supposed to take? (Twelve)

819. Who name went on the rod of Levi? (Aaron)

820. What would happen to the rod that the LORD chose? (Blossom

821. What happen to Aaron's rod was amazing? (The rod bloomed, blossom, and budded and brought forth almonds.)

822. Did this settle the murmuring among the crowd? (Yes)

823. What was the charge of the Levites? (To keep the tabernacle.)

824. How long was the charge of the Levites? (Forever

825. What does the LORD tell us about opening the matrix? (The first belong to Him whether man or beast.)

826. Why did Miriam die at? (Desert of Zin)

827. Why did the congregation chide with Moses? (There was no water.)

828. What did the LORD tell Moses to do? (Speak to the rock.)

829. How many times did Moses smote the rock? (Twice)

830. Was the LORD sanctify before the eyes of the children of Israel? (No)

831. Why not? (Moses didn't speak the words of sanctification before the struck the rock.)

832. What wouldn't the LORD let Moses and Aaron do to finish their journey? (They could not bring the children to the land which He had given them.)

833. What was the name of the waters? (Meribah)

834. What did Moses say to the king of Edom? (Can we pass through the king's high way.)

835. What was the king's answer? (No we will come out against you.)

836. What mount was Moses and Aaron when the LORD spoke about Aaron being gather to his people? (Mount Hor.)

837. What was the LORD to have Moses to do to Aaron? (Strip him of his garments.)

Journey Into Transjordon

838. Did Aaron die on the mount? (Yes)

839. Who got his garments? (His son, Eleazar)

840. How long did the congregation mourn Aaron? (Thirty days

841. Did king Arad fight against Israel? (Yes)
842. Did Israel vowed a vow for the LORD to deliver them into their hands? (Yes)
843. Did Israel utterly destroy their cities? (Yes)
844. What was the name of that place called? (Hormah)
845. Why were the people much discouraged? (There is no water or bread for their soul loathed the manna.)
846. Why did the LORD send out fiery serpents to bite the people? (They murmur and complained about the manna and having no water as if they didn't think by now the LORD could provide for them.)
847. What did the people want Moses to do for them? (Pray)
848. Did Moses pray for the people? (Yes)
849. Did the LORD hear his prayed? (Yes)
850. What did the LORD tell Moses to do for the people? (Make a fiery serpent, and set it upon a pole; everyone that looks upon it will live.)
851. When the children of Israel beheld the serpent what happen? (When any man that was bitten beheld the brass serpent they lived.)
852. What song did the people sang at the well? (Spring up, O well; sing you unto it.
853. What did the nobles did the well with? (Staves)
854. What was the king's name to whom they sent messengers too? (Si`hon king of the Amorites)
855. What did they ask the king of Amorites? (Let me pass through the land.)
856. Would Sihon king of the Amorites let the people pas through? (No)
857. Did they have to battle the Amorites? (Yes)
858. Who won the battle? (Moses and the people)
859. Was there a proverb about the place called Hesbon? (Yes)
860. Did the people dwell in the cities? (Yes)
861. What was the next city they conquer? (Bashan)
862. What was the name of the king? (Og king of Bashan)
863. What was the name of the battle? (Edrei)

864. What did the LORD say to Moses about the battle? (He has delivered the king and his people into Israel hand.)

865. Did they smote all the people in the kingdom of Og? (Yes)

866. Why was Balak, son of Zippor distressed? (He saw what they had done to the Amorites)

867. What did Balak want the Balaam to do to the people of Israel? (curse them)

868. What did he fear most about the children of Israel? (They cover the face of the earth.)

869. Why did Balak ask Balaam to curse the children of Israel? (He knew who Balaam bless would be blessed and whom he curse would be cursed.)

870. What did the LORD ask Balaam? (What men are these with you?)

871. What did the LORD say to Balaam? (Thou shall not go with them, curse not the people, for they are blessed.)

872. Did Balaam listen to the LORD? (No)

873. What do the story tell us Balaam motive? (He should listen to the LORD, because he is a prophet.)

874. Did Balak send again to entice Balaam? (yes)

875. What did the LORD say to Balaam? (If the men come go with them and speak only the words I tell you.)

876. Afterward, why did the LORD anger kindled against Balaam? (At the first the LORD had told Balaam not to go with the men.)

877. Who came out to meet Balaam in the way? (An angel)

878. What happen to the donkey that Balaam was riding? (He would not move because he saw the angel.)

879. How many times did Balaam smote the ass? (three)

880. Why did the ass not move in the direction that Balaam wanted him to? (The ass saw the angel.)

881. What was the reason the angel was sent out? (To slay Balaam for disobeying the LORD command.)

882. What made Balaam angry at the ass? (The ass struck his foot against the wall.)

883. Was the ass male or female? (female)

884. What did the LORD open for the ass? (her mouth)

885. What was their conversation like? (The ass ask a question about why Balaam had hit her three times.)

886. What was Balaam response? (You have mocked me these times.)

887. What would he had done to her if he had a sword? (He said he would have killed her.)

888. Why did the LORD open Balaam eyes? (To see the angel who had a sword.)

889. What did Balaam do when he saw the angel? (He bowed down his head, and fell flat on his face.)

890. What did the angel say to Balaam? (Wherefore have you smitten the ass these three times?)

891. What was Balaam response to the angel of the LORD? (For I have sinned, I knew not that thou stoutest in the way against me: now therefore, if it displease thee, I will get back again.)

892. What was the angel word unto Balaam? (Only the word that I shall speak unto thee, that shall thou speak.)

893. Who went out to meet Balaam? (Balak)

894. When Balak told Balaam I have power to promote thee to honor? (Balaam said I have not power to say anything but the word God put in my mouth, that shall I speak.)

895. Where was the place that they went to? (Kir`jath-hu`zoth)

896. They went up to a high place, what could Balaam see? (Utmost part of the people.)

897. What did Balaam tell Balak to build and prepare? (Build seven alters and prepare seven oxen and seven rams.)

898. Did the LORD put a word into Balaam mouth? (Yes, He spoke a parable.)

899. Did Balaam curse the children or bless them? (He blessed them altogether.)

900. Balak was not with understanding, He still wanted the people cursed. Would that happen to the children of Israel? (No)

901. Balak had Balaam to build a second alters and offer the same bullock and ram in sevens, Did he succeed at his mission? (No. Balaam told Balak what the LORD had spoken which was another parable.)

902. What happen the second burnt offering? (A bigger blessing came forth out of the mouth of Balaam.)

903. What is that famous scripture in Numbers chapter 23 verse 19? (God is not a man, that He should lie, neither the son of man that He should repent, hath He said, and shall He not do it? Or hath He spoken, and shall He not make it good?)

904. Where did Balak tell Balaam to go ? (The top of Peer.)

905. What did he ask Balaam to do for the third time? (Build seven alters and offer seven bullock and seven rams.)

906. When Balaam saw that it please the LORD to bless Israel what did he do? (He set his ace toward the wilderness.)

907. What happen to Balaam at this place? (The Spirit of the God came upon him.)

908. What happen next to Balaam? (He fell into a trance and spoke the word of God.)

909. What was Balak thoughts about the blessing? (These three times you have bless them instead of cursing go to your place?)

910. What nation did Israel begin to commit whoredom with? (Moab)

911. What did the LORD say for Moses to do to the people? (Hang them up before the LORD against the sun.)

912. What was the name of the man that thrust through the belly of the woman and man who brought her into his tent? (Phineas, the son of Eleazar)

913. How many die in the plaque? (Twenty and four thousand)

914. What major reward did Phineas receive from the LORD? (A covenant of peace)

915. How long will that covenant of peace last? (A covenant of an everlasting priesthood.)

916. What was the name of the daughters of Zelophehad names? (Mahlah, Noah, and Hoglah, and Micah, and Tirzah.)

917. Why did they stand before Moses? (Their father had no sons.)

918. What did they want from Moses and Eleazar the priest? (Their inheritance)

919. What did Moses do for them? (He took the cause to the LORD)

920. What did the LORD say about the inheritance? (They were right in speaking. The inheritance would pass on to them.)

921. Moses time would end soon. He need to set a man over the congregation who would be that man? (Joshua, son of Nun)

922. He would have to do this in front of the congregation? (Eleazar the priest and the congregation watched as Joshua receive the charge.)

923. What did the LORD command the children of Israel about His offering? (Two lambs of the first year without spot day by day for a continual burnt offering. One lamb in the morning and one lamb in the evening; and tenth part of an ephah of flour for a meat offering mingled with the fourth part of a hin) beaten oil. It is a continual burnt offering for a sweet savor, a sacrifice made by fire unto the LORD. And the drink offering shall be the fourth part of a hin for one lamb: in the holy place cause strong wine to be poured unto the LORD for a drink offering.)

924. What did He say for the Sabbath? (Two lambs of the first year without spot, and two tenth deals of flour for a meat offering, mingled with oil, and the drink offering thereof.)

925. What should happen in the seven month? (holy convocation)

926. What happens on that day? (no work and the blowing of trumpets.)

927. What happens on the tenth day of the seventh month? (Holy convocation, afflict your souls and do not do any work.)

928. When we vow a vow to the LORD we shall not break it? (we can not revise it)

929. Who can disallow a vow? (The father and the husband.)

930. What vows can the husband disallow? (Every vow)

931. What will be if the husband hold his peace? (The vow will stand.)

932. How old is the woman if the vow stays? (In her youth)

933. What vow of a widow and she that is divorced shall stand? (every vow they make shall stand.)

934. What are these vows called? (statutes)

935. What did the LORD say to Moses about the Midianite? (Avenge the children of Israel.)

936. What would happen next? (Moses would be gathered unto thy people or die.)

937. How many was armed for war? (Twelve thousand for war)

938. How many men from every tribe? (thousand.)

939. Did the priest go to the war? (Yes, Eleazar was priest)

940. Why did the priest go to the war? He had holy instruments, a trumpet to blow in his hand.)

941. Who did the men of war kill first? (males)

942. Did the kill the kings of Midian? (yes)

943. Why was Moses wroth with the officers of the host? (They saved the women alive.)

944. Why did Moses tell them to kill all the women that lay with men? They had caused the children to Israel to commit trespass against the LORD through the counsel of Balaam.)

945. Did Moses tell them to kill the little males? (Now therefore kill every male among the little ones, and kill every woman that hath known man by lying with him.)

946. How many days would the men of war have to stay outside the camp? (seven)

947. Did the captive have to be purify? (yes0

948. What else had to be purify? (raiment or clother)

949. What part of the law does purification follow under? (Ordinance)

950. What would make the gold, silver, brass, and tin and lead clean? Pass through the fire.)

951. Everything that would not stand fire would go through the water.

952. What day would they have to wash their clothes? (on the seventh day)

953. How did the LORD ask Moses to divide the prey? (two parts)

954. What was the way Moses divided it? (Between them that took the war upon them and the congregation.)

955. Note: A great teaching about atonement for the souls by giving offering to the LORD for when they battle into war and get monies give it to Jesus for the atonement of the souls of the men that go to battle to relieve suffering of the mind, emotions, and senses to set the captive free of emotional stress. What a blessing to discover the truth about psychology and freedom counseling of the mind. Thank You, LORD. A book about the truth of the atonement.

956. What is a booty? (prey taken from war)

957. What is a tribute? (tax)

958. What is a beeves? (cattle)

959. What is a soul? (person)

960. What portion shall the Levites get? (one portion of fifty of persons, beeves, asses, and of the flocks, of all manner of beasts.)

961. What was the job of the Levites? (To keep the charge over the tabernacle of the LORD.)

962. What is the purpose of the memorial? (Remembrance to the LORD.)

963. What two tribes wanted the land of Jazer and Gilead? (Reuben and Gad)

964. Why did they want the land? (They had much cattle and it was place for cattle.)

965. Did they ask Moses for the land? (yes)

966. What was Moses thoughts about the situation? (The agreement would stand as long as they went to battle with the others for their land.)

967. What would Moses let them do for their women and cattle? (build sheepfolds and cities)

968. Did this thing please Moses? (Yes, they would still have to come to war until their brethren inherited their places.)

969. What did Moses say would make them guiltless before the LORD? (Keeping their spoken word out of their own mouths.)

970. Who told Moses to write their goings out according to their journeys? (The LORD)

971. Of all the places they pitched in, what was different about Elim? (In Elim were twelve fountains of water and three-score and ten palm trees.)
972. How old was Aaron when he died? (Hundred and twenty-three)
973. What was the land of their inheritance? (The land of Canaan.)
974. What way should they inherit the land? (by lots)
975. What is the suburbs? (open land)
976. What is the city of refuge? (A place for a slayer, who kills unintentionally.)
977. What is a sojourner? (temporary resident)
978. What is a murderer? (A person, who decides in his heart,to smite another with iron, stone, or wood.)
979. What should happen to this person? (According to the law of Moses this person will surely be put to death.)
980. Where can the avenger of blood smite the murderer? (Outside the city of refuge.)
981. How long must the slayer remain in the city of refuge (until the death of the high priest)
982. How many witnesses do it take to put a man to death? (two or more)
983. What is the only way not to pollute the land of blood? (By the blood of him that shed it.)
984. Why are we not to defile the land? Because the LORD dwell in the land.)
985. What was about the daughters of Zelophehad's inheritance?)They had to marry the sons of their father's tribe.)
986. Which tribe was their father's tribe? (The son of Manasseh, the son of Joseph.)
987. Why can't the inheritance they marry out of the tribe of the fathers? (The inheritance could not move from tribe to tribe so, each could enjoy the inheritance of their fathers.)
988. Why was they only talking to the daughters? (Because their father had no sons.)
989. What shall happen during jubilee? (The land returns back to the original tribe.)
990. Did the daughters of Zelophehas obey Moses? (yes)

991. What would have happen if the disobeyed? (They would have no inheritance.)
992. Where were the children of Israel dwelling? (In the plains of Moab by Jordon near Jericho.)

Deuteronomy chapters 1-34

993. How many years did they spend in the wilderness and other places? (forty years)
994. Who are known as the patriarches? (Abraham, Isaac, and Jacob.)
995. Who told the people they were as stars of heaven for multitude? (Moses)
996. How many times are they more than before? (thousand time more)

First Address of Moses

997. What did Moses charge the Judges to do? (They should not respect persons in judgment; but hear small and great, not be afraid of face of man; bring Moses the hard judgments.)
998. Why do you think the people thought that God hated them? (We must have faith that God loves us. He proved us with Jesus.)
999. Who was the last kingdom of the giants? (Og king of Bashan)
1000. How long was his bed? (His bedstead was of iron and nine cubits in length and four cubits in breadth.)

Historical and Transitional Statement

1001. Did you know that the ten commandments are a covenant? (Yes)
1002. Did the LORD let Moses go over the Jordon to the Promised Land? (No)

1003. What person replaced Moses? (Joshua, son of Nun.)

1004. What kind of fire does the LORD consider Himself? (A consuming fire, even a jealous God.)

1005. What are other gods made of? (The work of men's hands, wood and stone, which neither see, nor hear, nor eat, nor smell.)

1006. What does the LORD warn us about other gods? (Don't serve them.)

1007. How can we find the LORD thy God? (Seek Him in our heart and soul.)

1008. Our God spoke out of midst of fire and they heard His voice what other god did this? (none other god)

1009. How did the LORD describe Himself? (Merciful)

1010. What are some of the great things that the LORD done for the people right in front of their faces? (God assayed to go and take Him a nation from the midst of another nation, by temptations, by signs, and wonders, and by war, and by a mighty hand and by a stretched out arm, and by great terrors, according to all that the LORD your God did for you in Egypt before your eyes.)

1011. What is one of the things that the LORD wants us to know for certainty? (There is none else beside Him.)

1012. When we keep the LORD's commandments and statutes what happens? (It prolongs our days upon the earth.)

1013. What must the people of God do with the commandments and statues? (Learn, keep and do them.)

1014. What did the LORD say He did for the Israelites? (He brought them out of Egypt from the house of bondage.)

The Second Address of Moses

1015. We shall have no other_____ before the LORD? (god)

1016. We should not make a _____. (graven image)

1017. We should not take the name of the LORD in _____. (vain)

1018. The _____ day is holy. (Sabbath)

1019. _____ thy father and mother so thy days will long upon the earth. (Honor)

1020. Thou shall not ____. (kill)

1021. Thou shall not commit _____. (adultery)

1022. Thou shall not _____. (steal)

1023. Thou shall not bear false _____, (witness)

1024. Thou shall not _____ anything that is thy neighbor.(covenant)

1025. How did the LORD speak to the assembly? (He spoke out of the midst of fire, with a great voice.)

1026. What did the LORD write on the two tablet of stone? (Ten Commandments)

1027. Did the assembly actually hear the LORD's voice? (yes)

1028. How did the mountains burn with fire? (A fire burn before the LORD for He says I am a consuming fire.)

1029. What was the assembly response to the LORD actions? (God showed His glory and His greatness and we have heard His voice out of the midst of the fire.)

1030. What was so awesome about His glory? (God talk with man, and He liveth.)

1031. Who is there of all flesh, that hath heard the voice of the living God speaking out of the midst of the fire? (We have and lived)

1032. What did the assembly ask Moses to do after they heard the LORD speaking? (Go thou near,and hear all that the LORD our God shall say and we will hear and do it.

1033. What did the LORD say to the assembly? (They have well said all that they have spoken.)

1034. What came from the LORD heart about the assembly feeling toward God ? (O if they were such a heart in the people that they would fear the LORD and keep His commandments always, that it might be well with their children forever.)

1035. What did the LORD tell the people to do? (Go you into your tents again.)

1036. What did He tell Moses to do? (Stand here thou by Me.)

1037. What was God main objective? (For all the people to learn and keep His commandments, statutes, and judgments into the land that He gave them.)

1038. What happen to the people before them? (They did not keep the commandments, statutes, or judgments or do them.)

1039. Why did the LORD come down from heaven to talk to the people? (To let them know that He was a God that talked and Love man.)

1040. before and He was the only, true living God and fear Him with a reverent fear.)

1041. What did the LORD say about Israel personally? (Hear, O Israel: the LORD our God is one LORD.)

1042. How should we love Him? (Love the LORD thy God with all thine heart, and with thine soul, and with all they might.)

1043. Where did He say the words should be? (in our heart)

1044. Should we teach them to our children? (yes)

1045. Should we talk about the words when we sittest in our house and go about the way.? (yes)

1046. When else should we keep the words? (When we lie down, and when thou rise up.)

1047. Do you know of any place the words should be that was not mentioned? (Bind the words upon thine hand and frontlet between thine eyes.)

1048. Is there anything that we did not mentioned? (Write them on the post of the house and the gate.)

1049. When we are in the houses full of good thing, what shall we do? (Remember the LORD thy God, who brought us out of the land of Egypt and the house of bondage.)

1050. What is a godly request from the LORD? (Fear and serve Him always and swear by His name.)

1051. They should not go after others round about them? (gods)

1052. What happen when the LORD anger is kindled against thee? (He will destroy thee from the face of the earth.)

1053. You should not tempt the LORD? (test)

1054. We are supposed to do right and good in the sight of the LORD? (Yes)

1055. When thou sons should say what mean the testimonies, and statutes, and the judgments which the LORD thy God commanded you? (Say we were Pharaoh's bondmen in Egypt and the LORD brought us out with a mighty hand.)

1056. What did the LORD do? (The LORD showed us signs and wonders great and sore, upon Egypt, upon Pharaoh, and upon all his household, before our eyes.)

1057. What promise did the LORD make to Abraham, Isaac and Jacob? (To bring them to the land that He swore to these patriarchs.)

1058. How is righteousness established? (When we observe to do all His commandments, before the LORD thy God as He commanded us.)

1059. What other nations were casted out so Israel could go in? (Hitites, and the Girgashites, and the Amorites, and the Canaanites, and the Perizzites, and the Hivites, and the Jebusites.)

1060. What was spoken about these nations? (Seven nations greater and mightier than thou.)

1061. What were they to do to these nations? (Smite them and utterly destroy them. Make no covenant with them and show them no mercy.)

1062. Why did the LORD say that they could not marry their daughters? (They would turn away thy son from following the LORD to serve other gods.)

1063. What should they destroy of these nations? (Destroy their altars, and break down their images, and cut down their groves, and burn their graven images with fire.)

1064. What did the LORD call the people of Israel? (A holy people, chosen and special unto Himself, above all the people on the face of the earth.)

1065. Why did the LORD set His love upon the people? (Because they would keep the oath He sworn unto their fathers.)

1066. Was there a lot of people in the beginning? (They were few in number.)

1067. What are some things that the LORD wants us to know about Him? (He is God, the faithful God which kept covenant and mercy with them that love Him and keep His commandments to a thousand generations.)

1068. What does the LORD do to the people that hate Him? (He repay them to their face to destroy them.)

1069. Are there benefits in keeping the commandments, statutes, and judgments to do them. (yes)

1070. What are the benefits? (H will love thee, and bless thee, and multiply thee: He will bless the fruit of thy womb, and the fruit of the land, thy corn, and thy wine, and thine oil, the increase of thy kind, and the flocks of thy sheep, in the land which he swore unto thy fathers to give thee. Thou shall be blessed above all the people: no barrenness among the male and female or in the cattle. Take sickness away from thee no evil disease of Egypt, which thou know, but lay them upon all that hate thee.)

1071. Do not say in thine heart that they are too strong and be afraid of them? (Remember what the LORD did unto Pharaoh and all Egypt.)

1072. What did the LORD say He will send among them to destroy them? (hornet)

1073. What did the LORD say about taking the silver or gold on graven images? (It is an abomination to the LORD thy God.)

1074. What is a cursed thing? (To bring an abomination into thine house.)

1075. Why should we keep His commandments? (So we can live and multiply and possess the land, Which He swore unto your fathers.)

1076. How did He find out what was in the heart of the people? (By leading them into the wilderness.)

1077. What did He find out? (Whether thou would keep His commandments, or no.)

1078. What was the purpose of manna? (To humble thee and suffer thee to hunger to make thee know that man do not live by bread only, but by every word that proceeded from the mouth of the LORD.)

1079. What was one of the miracle s they experienced in the wilderness? (Raiment or clothes did not wax old upon thee and foot didn't swell.)

1080. What are we asked to consider in our heart? (As a man chasteneth his son, so the LORD thy God chasteneth thee.)

1081. What was in the good land that the LORD brought them too? (A land of wheat, barley, and vines and fig trees and pomegranates, a land of oil olive and honey: A land wherein thou shall eat bread without scarceness, thou shall not lack any thing in it: a land whose stone is iron, and out of whose hills thou may dig brass.)

1082. What does it mean to bless the LORD? (Keeping His commandments, and His judgments, and His statutes, which I command thee this day.)

1083. What does it mean when He says thine heart be lifted up and you forget Me? (a person become proud hearted.)

1084. Why should we remember the LORD thy God? (He is the one that gives us power to get wealth.)

1085. What shall make a person say they have power and might in their hand to get wealth? (Not being

1086. What is God establishing? (His covenant which He swore unto thy fathers, as it is this day.)

1087. What was the name of some of the giants? (A`nak)

1088. Why did the LORD tell them to be not afraid? (He would go over before them as a consuming fire.)

1089. Why are they going in to possess the land? (For the wickedness of these nations the LORD do drive them out from before thee.)

Third Address of Moses

1090. What is another name for the ten commandments? (A table of covenant.)

1091. What did Moses say He did in the mount? (He abode there for forty days and forty nights. He eat neither bread nor drink water.)

1092. What did God use to write the ten commandments? (Finger of God.)

1093. What had the people made when Moses came down in anger? (molten image)

1094. What name did the LORD use to refer to the people? (stiff-necked)

1095. What did Aaron make while Moses was in the mount? (a golden calf)

1096. What did Moses to the calf? (Burn it with fire and ground it to dust and put it down the brook.)

1097. What happen at Taberah, and Massah, and at Kib`roth-hat-ta-`a-vah? (They provoked the LORD to anger.)

1098. What happen at Ka`desh-bar`ne-a? (They believed not the voice of the LORD.)

1099. Why should we not look at people stubbornness? (Looking to the promise keep us going in the right direction.)

1100. What did Moses tell the LORD to remember when he wanted to destroy the people for unbelief? (Moses said remember Abraham, Isaac, and Jacob.)

1101. Why did Moses think the people would say the LORD couldn't lead the people in the promise land? (Moses said the people would say because the LORD was not able to bring them into the land which He promised them, and because He hated them, He hath brought them out to slay them in the wilderness.)

1102. What did Moses have to do twice? (Hew thee two tables of stone like unto the first, and I will write on the tables the words that were in the first tables which thou broke.)

1103. What did the LORD write on the hewed two tables of stone? (He wrote on the tables, according to the first writing, ten commandments.)

1104. Why does Levi have no part with the brother's inheritance? (The LORD promised to be their inheritance when the tribe of the Levites did not participate in the golden calf, but was on the LORD's side.)

1105. Who is the Levites inheritance? (The LORD is his inheritance.)

1106. What does the LORD require of thee? (The LORD thy God require of thee, but to fear the LORD thy God, to walk in all His ways, and to Love Him, and to serve the LORD thy God with all thy heart and with all thy soul and to keep the commandments the LORD, and His statutes, Which I command thee this day for they good.)

1107. What belongs to the LORD? (Behold, the heaven and the heaven of heavens is the LORD's thy

1108. What has the LORD ask us to do? (Circumcise therefore the foreskin of your heart, and be no more stiff-necked.)

1109. Who is the LORD? (For the LORD your God is God of gods, and LORD of lords, a great God a mighty, and a terrible, which regarded not persons, nor taketh reward.)

1110. What does the LORD love to give the stranger? (food and clothes)

1111. Who does He execute judgment for? (fatherless and widow and stranger.)

1112. Who has the LORD ask us to love? (the stranger)

1113. Who shall we fear, serve and cleave too? (LORD thy God)

1114. What things have the LORD done for the people that they have seen? (Ten plaques on Pharaoh, and part the Red Sea, and the mount burnt with fire, water out of the rock and rain manna from heaven.)

1115. How many people went down in Egypt? (seventy person)

1116. How many people are there now? (The stars of heaven for multitude.)

1117. Why should they keep His requirement? (They shall always love the LORD thy God for taking them through difficult times and keep his charge and statutes, and His judgments.

1118. What are some more of the great acts of the LORD? (Dothan ad Abiam, the sons of Eliab, the son of Reuben: How the earth opened her mouth and swallowed them up, and their households and their tents, and all the substance that was in their possession.

1119. What are the benefits of obeying the LORD thy God in keeping the commandments? (He will give us rain of your land in its due season, the first rain and the latter rain, thou may gather in corn, wine, and oil and send grass for thy cattle.)

1120. What will happen if thou turn aside and serve other gods and worship them? (The LORD shut up heaven and there be no rain.)

1121. Where shall we lay up the words of the LORD? (We shall lay up the words in our hearts and soul and bind them for a sign upon your hand that they be as frontlets between your eyes.)

1122. When we keep the commandments what are the results? (The LORD shall drive out nations from before you and ye shall possess greater nations and mightier than yourselves.)_

1123. What shall be a blessing? (If you obey the commandments of the LORD your God, which I command you this day.)

1124. What is the cursing? (If you obey not the commandments of the LORD your God, to go after other gods, which you have not known.)

1125. What mount shall the blessing go on? (mount Gerizim)

1126. What mount shall the cursing go on? (mount Ebal)

1127. What have they been ask to do to their enemies alters and graven images? (Destroy all the places, where in the nations which ye shall possess served their gods, upon the high mountains, and upon the hills and under every green tree overthrow their altars, and break their pillars, and burn their groves with fire: and ye shall hew down the graven images of their gods, and destroy the names of them out of that place.)

1128. What have they been ask to do to their LORD thy God? (Ye shall seek the LORD habitation and bring offering sacrifices, and tithes and vows and the firstling of your herds and flocks.)

1129. What are two flesh that the people may eat when they are in their gates? (Roebuck and hart) btlings of thy herds or of thy flock, nor any of thy vows offering of thine hand.)

1130. Where shall they eat or offer to the LORD? (The place where He chose to put His name.)

1131. How do the nations serve their gods? Every abomination which He hated have they done unto their gods even their sons and daughters they have burnt in the fire to their gods.)

1132. What if a prophet or dreamer says, Let us go after other gods and let us serve them what is happening in this case? (This proving whether or not ye love the LORD thy God with all thy heart and with all your soul.)

1133. What shall happen to that prophet or dreamer? (He shall be put to death, because he has spoken to turn you away from the LORD your God.)

1134. What shall you do if another family member asks you to serve another god? (You shall not pity him or conceal him but surely put him to death.)

1135. How shall that person die? (Thy shall surely stone him with stones till he dies, because he sought to thrust thee away from the lord thy God.)

1136. What should happen if certain men and the children of Belial say let us go and serve other gods? (Thou shall inquire, and if it be true thou shall surely smite the inhabitants of the city with the edge of the sword.)

1137. What should you do with the spoil? (You should gather it into the street, and burn it with fire.)

1138. What can you not do for the dead? (Do not cut yourself or make any baldness between your eyes.)

1139. What would happen if you ate an abominable thing? (You would become sick and die.)

1140. What animals are considered abominable? (Swine, camel, hare, Coney)

1141. What are the beast that you should eat? (Ox, sheep, goat, hart, roebuck, fallow deer, wild goat, pygarg, and the mountain goat.)

1142. What is seethe? (Boil)

1143. What does it mean to no seethe a kid in its mother's milk? (Do not boil it.)

1144. What shall we eat of dead things? (Ye shall no eat of anything that dies of itself)

1145. Who may eat anything that dies of itself? (Give it to the stranger, or sell it to the alien.)

1146. If the place the Lord chose to eat at what shall a person do? (Turn it into money, bind up the money, and go to the place which the Lord thy God chooses.)

1147. What should be done at the end of the three years? (You should lay the increase within you gates and the Levite, stranger, fatherless and widow shall come and eat and be satisfied. And the Lord thy God shall bless the work of you hand.)

1148. What is the Lord's release? (After seven years every credition that lendeth to his neighbor, shall release it, not exact it of his neighbor.)

1149. Who can they exact of? (Foreigner)

1150. What is the blessing concerning this matter? (The promise is to lend unto many nations and not borrow.)

1151. What shall be done for the poor? (Lend sufficient for his needs.)

1152. What did God say about having wicked thoughts in your heart about the poor man? (Unless he cried to the Lord and it be sin unto thee.)

1153. What should you do? (Surely give him, then God will release a blessing thee in all thy works and in all that thou put thy hand unto.)

1154. Who shall not cause out of the Lord? (The poor.)

1155. When a Hebrew man or woman serve thou six years upon the seventh year what shall you do? (Let them go form thee free, and not empty handed.)

1156. What should you give him? (Flocks, wine, and all other things that thou have with thee.)

1157. What if they don't want to leave? (Take and aul and thrust it through his ear unto the door.)

1158. What are to be done with firstling males of thy herd and flock? (Sanctify unto the Lord thy God and don't work them.)

1159. What are these beast for? (To eat before the Lord thy God year by year in the place that the Lord should choose in the household.)

1160. If a beast is lame, blind, or blemished is found what do you do with it? (Don't sacrifice itmh4 unto the Lord.)

1161. What should happen to the blood? (Pour it upon the ground as water.)

1162. What month did they come out of Egypt? (A'bib)
1163. What month is the Passover? (A'bib)
1164. Was it day or night when the people came out of Egypt? (Night)
1165. What is the Passover? (Celebration of being led out of Egypt and blood taken from the Lamb to put over the door to keep the death angel passing over their house.)
1166. How many days shall the Passover be? (Seven)
1167. What kind of bread shall they eat? (unleavened bread)
1168. How long shall they remember coming out of Egypt? (All the days of their lives.)
1169. How shall the meat for the Passover be prepared (roasted)
1170. Should they do any work on the Passover? (No)
1171. What should be their attitude?) Joyful and rejoicing)
1172. What is the feast of weeks called? (The Feast of weeks is called Pentecost)
1173. How many times a year should the males appear before the LORD thy God? (Three times a year)
1174. What are the times they should appear? (Passover: unleaven bread, feast of the weeks, and feast of the tabernacle.)
1175. What is the feast of tabernacle? (Seven days after thou gather corn and wine.)
1176. How should every man give? (Every man give as he is able, according to the blessing of the LORD thy God, which he have given them.)
1177. What is a judge? (A person who judges between right and wrong.)
1178. Who shall not take a bribe? (Judge or officer)
1179. What is an officer? (He is a man assigned to carry out judgment.)
1180. What is a bribe? (A gift to twist the just.)
1181. Where should you not plant a grove of trees? (Near the altars of the LORD thy God.)
1182. What is an abomination of sacrificing to the LORD? (A bullock or sheep with a blemish or blindness and lame.)

1183. What happen to men and women that serve other gods or transgress the covenant? (They are to be stoned with stone.)

1184. What is the first thing to do to find out information about the situation? (Enquire diligently to know the truth.)

1185. How many witness must you have? (Two or three)

1186. What happen when a judgment it too hard? (Enquire of the Priest, of Levites and the judge of that day.)

1187. What is something the king is asked not to do? (Multiply horses and return to Egypt.)

1188. What other things must the not multiply to himself? (Wives, silver and gold.)

1189. Where should the king come from? (Among thy brothers)

1190. What law shall the king write? (Not to multiply wives, silver and gold to himself.)

1191. How many days should he read the law? (All the days of his life.)

1192. What shall he learn to do? (Fear the LORD thy God, to keep all the words of this law and statutes to do them.)

1193. What kind of heart shall a king have? (Merciful heart)

1194. What offering should the Levite eat? (The LORD's offering made by fire.)

1195. What part of the ox and sheep should the priest eat? (Shoulder, two cheeks and maw.)

1196. What are some of the first fruit? (Corn, wine and oil, first of the fleece of sheep.)

1197. How long are the Levites chosen to minister to the LORD thy God? (They are chosen forever.)

1198. What is patrimony? (Estates)

1199. What is a pagan rite? (To make your son or daughter pass through the fire.)

1200. What is divination? (Fortune telling)

1201. What is a enchanter? (magician)

1202. What is a familiar spirit? (Spells)

1203. What is a wizard? (Medium)

1204. What is a necromancer? (Consults the dead)

1205. Who shall God's people listen too? (A prophet of God.)

1206. Who shall hear the LORD's prophet? (Everyone)

1207. Will the LORD require the words spoken by the prophet? (Yes)

1208. What shall the people not remove? (Landmarks of old.)

1209. Who shall not go into battle? (A man who have built a new house and have not dedicated it, a man who planted a vineyard and betrothed a wife.)

1210. What are tributaries? (Forced labor)

1211. What group of people shall they destroy? (Hittites, Amorites, Canaanites, and Perizzites, Hivites, and Jebusites.)

1212. Why kill all these people? (So that they cannot teach you to do after all the their abominations which they have done to their gods.)

1213. When you besiege a city. Why should you not cut down the trees? (You may eat of them, the trees are the man's life.)

1214. Who shall be called when a man is slain in a field? (The elders and the judges.)

1215. When a beautiful woman is taken captive and he wants her to be for a wife, what must take place? (Shave her head, pare her nails and change clothes remain in his home and bewail her father and mother a full month.)

1216. What portion must the first born receive? (Double portion)

1217. If a man has two wives and one are beloved and one hate. They both have sons and the hated has his firstborn. Who will receive the inheritance first? (Firstborn of the hated.)

1218. When you have a stubborn and rebellious son. What shall be done? (Bring him to the elders of the city.)

1219. What will happen when the son will not obey their voice and is a glutton and drunkard? (Stone him with stones until he dies.)

1220. When a man commit a sin worthy of death and they hang him on a tree. What happen? (He must not be allowed to hang over night.)

1221. Why must he not remain overnight? (He is accused of the LORD.)

1222. What should you do seeing your brother ox or sheep go astray? (Bring it back to him.)

1223. What if you don't know him? (Keep the beast at your house until he come seeking it.)

1224. What would you do to his clothes or ass or anything belonging to him? (Keep all the things to his home until he seeks it.)

1225. Why must we be responsible for our brethren? (For the LORD thy God is holy.)

1226. Why should you help the brethren lift his ox or ass? (We are commanded to do so by the law.)

1227. Should a woman wear men's clothing? (No)

1228. Should a man wear women clothing? (No)

1229. Why should they not wear each other clothing? (It is an abomination before the LORD thy God.)

1230. What should you do when building a new house? (Make a battlement for it.)

1231. How should you sow a vineyard? (With one type of seed.)

1232. What is divers seed? (Various seed)

1233. Would mixed seed defile your vineyard? (Yes)

1234. How shall you plow the beast? Don't plow with an ox and ass together.)

1235. What garments shall not be worn together? (Woolen and linen)

1236. What is the situation when a man takes a wife and goes into her and hate her? (If she is a virgin the man must pay the father and mother hundred shekels of silver. If she isn't a virgin she must be stoned.)

1237. When a man be found lying with a married woman. How is the outcome? (They both are stoned with stones until death.)

1238. What happen when a damsel is betrothed a man and another man lies with her? (Bring them out of the gate of the city that they both be stoned with stone to death.)

1239. How many fringes should be on thy vesture? (Two)

1240. What happen when man finds a betrothed damsel in a field and force her and lie with her? (The man should die.)

1241. When a man finds a damsel in a field that is a virgin which is not betrothed to a man and lie with her what happens? (He should give her father fifty shekels of silver and marry the woman.)

1242. How should a son treat his father's wife? (He must not take his father wife, or discover his skirt.)

1243. Who should not enter into the congregation of the LORD? (A bastard until the tenth generation.)

1244. What is a bastard? (An illegitimate child.)

1245. Can an Amorite and Moabite enter into the congregation of the LORD? (Can't enter the congregation forever.)

1246. Why must they not enter in the congregation? (Because he meets you not with bread and water, and hired Balaam to curse you.)

1247. Would God listen to Balaam? (No. He turned the curse into a blessing.)

1248. Why do you think He did this? (The LORD thy God love us)

1249. What two things must they not seek for the Amorites and Moabites? (Their peace and prosperity.)

1250. Who must thy not abhor? (Edomite and Egyptians)

1251. What should they not be abhorred? (Edomite is thy brethren and they were strangers in Egypt.)

1252. When can their children enter into the congregation? (Third generation)

1253. What must happen when a host goes forth against the enemies? (Keep them from every wicked thing.)

1254. What must unclean men do in the camp? (He must wash himself with water and at even when the sun goes down he will be clean. Then come into the camp.)

1255. What should be done when men go to the bathroom at war? (You must take a paddle with you to cover with.)

1256. Why should it be covered? (The LORD thy God is in the midst of the camp to deliver thee, therefore the camp must be holy.)

1257. Why should not return a escaped servant to his master? (He should not be oppress, let him stay where he like the best.)

1258. What person should not be in the daughters of Israel? (A whore)

1259. What person should not be in the sons of Israel? (A sodomite)

1260. What should you not bring into the house of the LORD thy God? (Bring not the price of a whore for a vow, and the price of a dog,)

1261. What are they both before the LORD thy God? (An Abomination.)

1262. Why should you not lend usury upon the brethren? (That the LORD thy God may bless all that thine sittest unto in the land whither thy go to possess It.?

1263. What is usury? (Interest)

1264. Who shall you lend usury too? (Stranger)

1265. What will the LORD thy God do for you? (Bless you)

1266. How should you keep a vow to the LORD thy God? (Be not slack in the paying that vows for the LORD thy God will surely require it of you.)

1267. What if you forbear to pay it? (That will be sin.)

1268. What if you forbear to vow? (It is no sin.)

1269. What we vow with our mouth we must do? (That which is gone out of your lips thou shalt keep and perform.)

1270. What happen when you come into your neighbor vineyard and the grapes are ripe? (You can eat to fill but not put into a vessel.

1271. What happen when you come to corn? (When the corn is standing get some in your hand.)

1272. Can you move a sickle in standing corn? (No)

1273. Can a man that has a wife find uncleanness in her give her a bill of divorcement? (Yes)

1274. Can she become another man's wife? (Yes)

1275. Can a person marry the same person twice? (No)

1276. Can you marry a former husband, if the latter husband dies? (No)

1277. Why can't you do this? (That person would be defiled, and it is an abomination before the LORD thy God.)

1278. What shall happen when a man take a new wife at wartime? (He shall be free at home to cheer up her for one year.)

1279. Can you steal your brethren and sell him? (The thief shall die.)

1280. How can you avoid the plaque of leprosy? (Do according to all the priest and Levite teach you.)

1281. What is a pledge? (Security for debt.)

1282. What will happen if you give a man his pledge before the sun goes down? (The LORD thy God will bless you. It will be righteous before the LORD thy God.)

1283. What will happen if you oppress the hire servant?)if he cries out to the LORD thy God and it be sin to thou.)

1284. How do you handle this kind of sin? (Every man pays for his own sin)

1285. Who must bear his own sin? (The father cannot be put to death for the children, and the children cannot be put to death for the father.)

1286. Can you pervert the judgment of a stranger nor of the fatherless, nor of the widow's clothes to pledge? No)

1287. Who is commanding us not to pervert the judgment of the stranger, fatherless and widow? (The LORD thy God commands us to do this thing.)

1288. Why must thou not go over the fields to get a sheaf in the harvest? (You must leave it for the stranger, fatherless and widow.)

1289. What is the blessing for doing this? (The LORD thy God will bless the work of thy hand.)

1290. What has the LORD ask them to do in harvest concerning the olive trees, grapes? (Leave some for the stranger, fatherless and widow.)

1291. What shall thou remember? (When thou was a bondman if the land of Egypt. This is a commanded thing)

1292. Can you muzzle the ox when he treaded the corn? (No)

1293. What is a controversy? (Dispute)

1294. What happen in a controversy? (They shall justify the righteous and not the wicked.)

1295. How many stripes must the wicked receive? (forty stripes)

1296. What happen when the brethren refuse to take her to wife? (He will be brought before the elders of the city, the brother's wife shall loose his shoes from his feet and spit in his face and say, It will be done to the brother who will not build up his brother household.)

1297. What shall his name be called in Israel? (The house of him that has his shoe loosed.)

1298. What happen when two men strive and his wife deliver him by grabbing the other man secrets (genitals)? (She must have her hand cut off without pity.)

1299. What are divers? (Different)

1300. When you are in the land to possess it what should you do? (Take the first of the fruit of the earth to the place the LORD chose.)

1301. What should the people confess? (We are come into the country the LORD swore to give our fathers.)

1302. When you have given the priest the basket at the altar. What shall you say? (A Syrian ready to perish was my father, went down to Egypt, sojourned a few, become there a mighty great nation and populous, And the Egyptians evil treated us, and afflicted us, and laid upon us hard bondage: And when we cried unto the LORD God of our fathers, the LORD heard our voice, and looked on our affliction, and our labor, and our oppression: And the LORD brought us forth with a mighty hand with outstretched arm, and with great terribleness, and with signs and with wonders: And He hath brought us into the place and hath given us this land, even a land that flowed with milk and honey. And thou have brought to the first fruits which Thou, O LORD have given me. And thou shall set it before the LORD thy God and worship there and rejoice in every good thing which the LORD thy God hath given thee and thy house and the Levite, and the stranger that is among you.)

1303. What year shall thy bring all the tithes of thine increase? (Third)

1304. What is the year of tithing? (Third)

1305. Who shall thy give it too? (Levite, the stranger, the fatherless and widow.)

1306. Where shall they eat it? (Within the gated and be filled.)

1307. Who must you give the hallowed things too? (The Levites, stranger, fatherless and widow.)

1308. What must we do to keep the commandments? (Do not transgress or forget them.)

1309. What will the LORD thy God do for the people? (Bless them)

1310. When the people say to the LORD thy God is my God and He says you are my people what has taken place? (We are his peculiar people.)

1311. Will he make us a holy people? (Yes)

1312. What are a peculiar people? (Treasured possession)

1313. When they pass over Jordon unto the land that the LORD thy God give them, thou shall set up great stones and plaster them. What shall they write on the stones? (All the words of the law.)

1314. What mount shall they bless the people? (Gerizim)

1315. What tribes shall be there to bless? (Simeon, Levi, Judah, Issachar, Joseph and Benjamin.)

1316. What mount shall they stand to do the curses? (Ebal

1317. What tribe shall stand on Mount Ebal to curse? (Reuben, Gad, Asher Zebulun, Dan, and Naphtha-li.)

1318. What is one of the curses? (Cursed be the man that makes graven images.)

1319. What is one on the blessing? (Hearken unto the voice of the LORD thy God, do all His commandments, which I command thee this day, that the LORD thy God will set thee on high above all nations of the earth: And all these blessings shall come on thee, and take over thee, if thou shall hearken voice of the LORD thy God.)

Deuteronomy Chapters 28-34

1320. How do you receive a blessing from the LORD? (Hearken diligently to the voice of the LORD and do all His commandments.)

1321. What does the blessing do to the person? (Overtake thee.)

1322. What does blessing mean? (Empowered to prosper.)

1323. What is the does hearken mean? (To obey or listen)

1324. What does overtake mean? (Run you over.)

1325. How many blessing was in Deuteronomy chapter 28? (Fourteen)

1326. How many curses? (Fifty-three)

1327. What does curse mean? (Empowered to fail)

1328. How does a person get a curse? (Result of disobedience)

1329. How does a person get a blessing? (The results of obedience)

(BLESSING)

1330. What will overtake a person who hearken to the voice of the LORD thy God? (All these blessings shall come on thee and overtake thee.)

1331. Where will a person be blessed? (Blessed shall thou be in the city and the field.)

1332. What are of some of the personal blessings? (Blessed shall be the fruit of the body, and the fruit of thy ground, and the fruit of the cattle, the increase of the kind, and the flocks of thy sheep.)

1333. What are other blessings? (Blessed shall be they basket and store.)

1334. How are thy blessings in thy goings? (Blessed shalt thou be when thou comes in, and when thou goes out.)

1335. What did the LORD say about the enemies? (The LORD shall cause thine enemies that rise against thee to be smitten before thy face: they shall come out against thee one way, and flee before thee seven ways.)

1336. Where will the LORD command His blessing? (The LORD will command the blessing upon thee in thy storehouses, and in all that thou set thine hand unto; and He shall bless thee in the land which the LORD thy God giveth thee.)

1337. What happens when you keep the LORD's commandments? (The LORD shall establish thee and holy people unto Himself, as He hath sworn unto thee, if thou keep the commandments of the LORD thy God, and walk in His ways.)

1338. How will people view you? (All the people of the earth shall see that thou art called by the name of the LORD: and they shall be afraid of thee.)

1339. How shall the LORD bless thee in goods? (The LORD shall make thee plenteous in goods, in the fruit of the body, and in the fruit of thy cattle, and in the fruit of the ground, in the land which the LORD swore unto thy fathers to give thee.)

1340. What is the LORD's good treasure? (The heaven to give the rain unto thy land in it season, and to bless all the work of thine hand; and lend unto many nations and sot borrow.)

1341. What is the leadership blessing? (The LORD shall make thee the head, and not the tail; and thou shalt be above only, and not beneath; if thou hearken and observe the commandments this day to do them.)

1342. What shall the people not turn aside and do? (Thou shall not turn aside from any of the words which I command thee this day, to the right hand, or to the left, to go after other gods to serve them

(CURSES)

1343. What will happen to the ones who will not hearken to the voice of the LORD thy God? (It shall come to pass if thy will not hearken unto the voice of the LORD thy God, to observe to do all the commandments, and His statutes which I command thee this day; that all these curses shall come upon thee, and overtake thee.)

1344. Where will thou be cursed first? (In the city and the field)

1345. Where else will thou be cursed? (Cursed in thy basket and store)

1346. What curse is kind of personal? (Cursed in the body, and fruit of the land, the increase in kind, and the flocks of thy sheep.)

1347. What happens in thy goings? (Cursed in thy coming in and curse in thy going out.)

1348. What happen to a person that forsake the LORD? (The LORD will send cursing, vexation, and rebuke, in all that thou sett thine hand to do, until thou be destroyed, and until thou perish quickly; because of the wickedness of thy doings, whereby thou hast forsaken Me.)

1349. What will the LORD make cleave to thee? (The LORD will make pestilence cleave unto thee, until He has consumed thee from off the land, thou goes to possess it.)

1350. What will the LORD smite thee with? (The LORD will smite thee with a consumption, and with a fever, and with an inflammation, and with an extreme burning, and with the sword, and with blasting, and with mildew, and they shall consume thee until thou perish.)

1351. What will heaven and earth is like to the curse? (The heaven that is over thy head shall be brass, and the earth that is under thee shall be iron.)

1352. What about the rain? (The LORD shall make the rain of thy land as powder and dust; from heaven shall it come down upon thee, until thou be destroyed.)

1353. What about your carcass? (Your carcass shall be meat for all the fowls of the air. The beasts of the earth and no man shall fray them away.)

1354. What is the botch of Egypt? (The LORD shall smite thee with the botch of Egypt, and with emer rods, and with the scab, and with an itch, whereof thou cannot be healed.)

1355. What about mental disorders? (The LORD will smite thee with madness, blindness, and astonishment of heart.)

1356. How shall thou act at noonday? (Thou shall grope at noonday, as the blind groped in darkness, and thou shalt not proper in thy ways; and thou shalt be only oppressed and spoiled evermore, and no man shall save thee.)

1357. What about a spouse? (Thou shall betroth a wife, and another man shall lie with her: thou shall build a house, and thou shalt not dwell therein; thou shall plant a vineyard and not gather the griped.

1358. What will happen to thy beasts? (Thine ox shall be slain before thine eyes, and thou shalt not eat thereof: thine ass shall be violently taken away from before thy face, and not be restored to thee: thy sheep shall be given to thy enemies, and not rescued.)

1359. What will happen to thy sons and daughters? (They shall be given to another people, and thine eyes shall look for them and fail longing for them all the day long, and there shall be no might in thine hand.)

1360. What will be thy emotions state? (Another nation shall eat up the fruit of thy land, which thou know not and thou shall be only oppressed and crushed.)

1361. What shall make thee mad? (Thou shall be mad for the sight of thine eyes which thou shalt see.)

1362. What is a sore botch? (The LORD shall smite thee in the knees, and in the legs, with a sore botch that cannot be healed, from the sole of thy foot unto the top of thy head, boil.)

1363. What will the LORD bring upon them? He will bring them to a nation unknown by their fathers, to serve other gods, wood and stone.)

1364. What will the people become? (The people will become an astonishment, a proverb, and a byword.)

1365. Who shall consume the fields? (The Locusts)

1366. What is a proverb? (Wise saying or precept about people.)

1367. What is astonishment? (Overpowering wonder or surprise; amazement.)

1368. What is a byword? (A word or phrase associated with a person or group.)

1369. Who will eat the grapes and drink the wine? (The Worms)

1370. What will happen to the olive trees? (Cast their fruit and lose it.)

1371. What shall happen to sons and daughters? (They shall go into captivity.)

1372. Who will devour all the fruit of the land? (The Locusts)

1373. What will the stranger do? (The stranger shall get above thee very high, and thou come down very low.)

1374. Who shall be the head? (The stranger)

1375. What is the head? (The important one)

1376. Why has all these things happen to them or us? (We didn't hearken to the voice of the LORD thy God, to keep his commandments and statues, which He commanded.)

1377. Why shall the curse be upon the people? (A sign and wonder, upon thy seed forever.)

1378. What is a wonder? (Miracle)

1379. What is a seed? (Descendants)

1380. Why should the curse be? (Thou didn't serve the LORD thy God with a joyfulness and gladness of the heart.)

1381. How shall we serve our enemies? (Hunger and thirst, nakedness, and in want of all things, with a yoke of iron on thy neck until they be destroyed.)

1382. Who will the LORD bring against them? (A nation as swift as the eagle, and a nation whose tongue they will not understand.)

1383. How will this nation be? (Fierce countenance, not regard the old person or show favor to the young person.)

1384. What will the nation destroy? (The fruit of the cattle, fruit of the land, leave no corn, wine or oil, destroy all the cattle and flocks of sheep.)

1385. What will the enemies cause the people to do to their own children? (They shall eat the fruit of their children body in their hardships.)

1386. What shall a brother that is evil toward his own family do? (He will refuse to share the flesh of his own children with his family.)

1387. What will the young women do to her family? (Eat he own children.)

1388. What shall the people fear? (The name that is glorious and fearful of the LORD THY GOD.)

1389. What is fearful in this sentence? (AWESOME)

1390. What kind plagues will the LORD thy God make? (Great plagues of long continuance and sore sicknesses of long continuance.)

1391. What is a plague? (Pestilence, illness)

If you believe in Jesus Christ you are redeemed from these curses. When He stepped down from glory it was for the people who would believe in Him. He went through the cross to save those wonderful people from every nation. To restore mankind, His beloved, and now I present to you all that Jesus have done for you. He has redeemed us from the curse of the law, being made a curse for us for it is written; curse is everyone who hang on the tree. Gal. 3:13) Don't worry about the curses, because the LORD JESUS CHRIST have already redeemed us from the curses, for it written curses is anyone who hangs on the tree. Gal. 3:13-14. Victory has been given us today and always. Faithful and true is HE.

1392. What will He do with the disease of Egypt? (Bring them upon the people until they be destroyed.)

1393. What will be the total outcome of the people? (They will be destroyed by disease and left few in number.

1394. Why ? (They obey not the voice of the LORD thy God.)

1395. Who will rejoice over them to destroythem and bring them to nought? (The LORD thy God.)

1396. What is nought? (Nothing)

1397. Who will scatter the people to the ends of the earth, from one end to the other, to server other gods wood and stone? (The LORD thy God)

1398. What is another part of the curse? (There is no rest for feet, a trembling heart, failing of the eyes and sorrow of mind.)

1399. Name some things that will happen to the people because of not obeying the LORD thy GOD? (Life shall hang in doubt,fear dayand night,none assurance of thy life.)

1400. What will the fearful say night and day?(In the morning they will say "would GOD it were even", in the even they will say" would GOD it were morning")

1401. What is the last curse? (The LORD shall bring these into Egypt again by ships. Thou shall see it no more again: and there ye shall be sold into your enemies for bondmen and bond women, no man shall buy you.)

1402. Have we seen some of these curses in a book of the bible before? (The book of the Job.)

1403. What do we call the blessing and cursing in Deuteronomy chapter 28:1-68? (A covenant)

1404. Where was the covenant made? (In the land of Moab.)

1405. Who commanded the covenant to be follow? (The LORD thy God.)

Moses Closing Days and Activities

1406.	What did the Moses say to the children of Israel? (You have seen all the LORD did before your eyes in the land of Egypt unto Pharoah, unto all his servants, unto all the land, great temptations, signs and miracles.)

1407.	What did Moses highlight to them? (The Lord have just given them eyes, ears and heart to perceive with this day.)

1408.	What is perceive? (To know or understand.)

1409.	What did they wear in the wilderness? (Your clothes have not waxen old upon you. They had the same clothes.)

1410.	What did they not eat? (No bread, wine or strong drinks that ye might know that I am the LORD your God.)

1411.	What did Moses tell them to do? (Keep the words of this covenant to do them, that ye may prosper in all that ye do.)

1412.	Who did partake of this covenant? (Everyone present that day.)

1413.	What is a covenant? (An agreement.)

1414.	Who else did He make the covenant with? (Those who was pesent and absent was apart of the covenant.)

1415.	How do they add drunkenness to thirst? (Say in their heart that they are blessed, walking in the curse, thinking about peace.)

1416.	What will the LORD do to this man or women? (All the curses written in this book shall lie upon him and the Lord shall blot out his name from under heaven.)

1417.	How shall the Lord separate the people? (According to all this curses written in this book of law.)

1418.	What shall the next generation say unto them? (What meaneth the heat of this great anger.)

1419.	What are the secrets things? (Hidden Realities)

1420.	What cities burnt with brimstones and salt? (Sodom and Gomorreh, Adman and Zeboim.)

1421. Can anything grow on the land again? (It will not sow, or bearth, nor any grass groweth therein.)

1422. What will men say about the heat of the great anger? (The people will say that they forsook the covenant that the LORD God made with them and their fathers when He brought them out of Egypt.)

1423. What is "call to mind" the blessing and the cursing? (Remember them.)

1424. Is their a blessing in returning to the covenant? (Yes, the LORD will turn thy captivity and gather thee from all the nations.)

1425. How will He bless thee? (He will dothem good and multiply thee above thy fathers.)

1426. What does circumcise mean? (To cut away from.)

1427. How will the LORD circumcise their hearts? (When they love the LORD thy God with all their heart, and with all they soul, that thy may live.)

1428. When the people obey the LORD thy God, Who will He put the curses on? (Their enemies who persecuted them and hated them.)

1429. When the people return, what will happen? (They will obey the voice of the LORD and do all His commandments this day.)

1430. What are some of the benefits of returning to obey His voice? (The LORD thy God will make the thee plenteous in every work of thine hand, in the fruit of the body, and in the fruit of the cattle, and in the fruit of the land.)

1431. Where are the commandments hidden, that we may not make excuses as to obey them. (The word is very nigh unto thee in thy mouth, and in thy heart, that thee mayest do it.)

1432. How shall the LORD react to the obedience? (He shall rejoice over thee as He rejoiced over thy fathers.)

1433. What choice have the LORD set before us this day? (Life and good, death and evil. He commanded us to love Him, walk in His ways, keep His commandments and His statues, and judgments that we may live and multiply,)

1434. Who do the Lord call to record this day against you? (Heaven and earth)

1435. What choice does set before us? (Life and death, blessing and cursing.)

1436. Which one should we choose? (Life and blessing)

1437. How old were Moses, when he couldn't go out and come in? (One Hundred and twenty)

1438. What did the LORD say to Moses about the Jordon river? (Thou shall not go over the Jordon.)

1439. Who would become their new leader? (Joshua)

1440. What was some of the kings that they had destroyed? (Sihon and Og, kings of the Amorites.)

1441. How did Moses encourage Joshua? (Be strong and of good courage, fear not for the LORD thy God will not fail thee, nor forsake thee.)

1442. Who shall cause the people to inherit the land? (Joshua)

1443. Who did Moses say would go before Joshua? (The LoRD thy God will be with thee and neither forsake thee : fear not, neither be discouraged.)

1444. Who did Moses give this law to? (The priests, sons of Levi, which bare the ark of the covenant.)

1445. What was the law? (The LORD would fight for them and destroy other nations and they shall possess them. Joshua was the new leader.)

1446. What did Moses command them saying (They shall read this law before all Israel in their hearing.)

1447. How many years? (Seven years)

1448. What shall happen on the seven year end? ((Year of release, in the feast of tabernacles.)

1449. Who shall gather together? (Men and women, and children and thy strangers that is within thy gates.)

1450. What must they learn? (Fear the LORD thy God, and observe to do all the words of this law.)

1451. How will the children learn? (They who have not known anything mau hear and learn to fear the LORD thy God, as long as they live in the land.)

1452. Why did the Lord call Moses? (He must die and sleep with his fathers.)

1453. How did the LORD appear in the tabernacle? (He appeared in the cloud and the cloud stood oner the door of the tabernacle.)

1454. What did the LORD say about the people? (The people will go a whoring after gods of srangers of the land and will forsake Hin and break covenant.)

1455. What will happen next? (The LORD will forsake them also.)

1456. What will the people say in that day? (These evil are come upon us because God is not among us.)

1457. Why did Moses write a song? (To be a witness against the children of Israel.)

1458. What did the LORD reveal about the people? (He knew their imaginations, before He brout them intgo the land.)

1459. What happen to Moses all in the same day? (Wrote the song the same day, and taught it to the children of Israel.)

1460. Who received a charge? (Joshua)

1461. What was Moses charge? (He shall bring the children of Israel into the land,)

1462. What did Moses command the Levites? (Take this book of the lawand put it in the side of the ark of the covenant of the LORD thy God, that it mauy be there for a witness againsy them.)

1463. What did Moses say he knew about their rebellions? (Their stiffnecks and rebellion againsg the LORD.)

1464. What was his instructions to them? (Gather all the elders of your teibes, officers that he may speeak the words to them.)

1465. What gods will they go after? (The gods they make with their hands.)

1466. How did the people provoke the LORD to jealousy? (Serving strange gods and abominations.)

1467. Who do vengeance belong to? (The LORD thy God)

1468. Who will recompence? (The LORD thy God)

1469. What does vengeance mean? (Infliction of a deserved pentalty.)

1470. What is recompence? (To repay for damages.)

1471. What did the LORD thy God say about Himself in the song? (There is no god with Me. I kill, and I make alive; I wound, and I heal: neither is there any that can deliver out of my hand.)

1472. What is Joshua other name? (Hoshe'a)

1473. What happened to Moses after he wrote the song? (It was his time to die.)

1474. Where was he buried? (The Mount Abarim unto Mount Ne'bo wich is in the land of Moab.)

1475. Why was Moses not allowed to cross the Jordon? (He did't sanctified the LORD in the midst of the children of Israel.)

1476. Was Moses allowed to see the land? (Yes)

1477. What tribe receive the first blessing? (Reuben)

1478. Who was next? (Judah)

1479. What does Judah mean? (Praise)

1480. What was special about Levi? (They observed thy word, and kept thy covenant.)

1481. What about Benjamin? (The beloved of the Lord shall dwell in safety by him, and the LORD shall cover him all day long, he shall dwell between his shoulder.)

1482. What about Joseph? (Blessed be his land of the LORD for the precious things of heaven, for the dew, for the deep that couched beneath. Ten thousands of sEphraim thouands of Manasseh.)

1483. What about Zebulun and Isschar? (Rejoice Zevbulun in thy goig out and Issachar)

1484. What did he say to God? (Blessed be he that enlarged God, He dwelleth as a lion and tearth the arm with a crow.)

1485. How about Dan? (Dan is a lion's whelp: he shall leap from Bashan.)

1486. How about Naph-tali? (Satisfied with favor and full with the blessing of the LORD possess the west and south.)

1487. What about Asher? (Let Asher be blessed with childre, let him be acceptable to his brethren and dip his foot in oil.)

1488. What special thing did the LORD do for Moses? (Before Moses slept with his fathers, He let Moses see the land that was theirs.)

1489. How long did the people weep for Moses? (Thirty days)

1490. What spirit did Joshua get from Moses, by the laying on hands? (The Spirit of Wisdom.)

1491. Was there a prophet like Moses? (The LORD knew Moses face to face in all Israel.)

1492. What offering is accepted by the LORD?

1493. What did Moses speak about the external concerning their enemies? (The external God is thy refuge, and underneath are the everlasting arms: and he shall thrust out the enemy from before thee; and shall say, Destroy them.)

1494. How shall Israel dwell before the LORD after Moses is dead? (Israel then shall dwell in safety alone:The fountain of Jacob shall be upon a land ofcorn and wine, also his heavens shall drop down dew.)

1495. Why did Moses say that Israel shall be Happy? (Happy art thou, O Israel who is like unto thee, O people saved by the LORD, the shield of thy help, and who is the sword of thy excellency! and thine enemies shall be found liar unto thee; and thou shall tread upon their high places.)

THANK YOU LORD